ON
LOVING
WOMEN

FOR CATHERINE, CHARLOTTE, JEANNE, MH, MARIE, MATHILDE, MAXIME, OCTOBER, AND SASHA.

ENTIRE CONTENTS © COPYRIGHT 2014 DIANE OBOMSAWIN. TRANSLATION © COPYRIGHT 2014 HELGE DASCHER, WITH SPECIAL THANKS TO KATE BATTLE, DAG DASCHER, AND ROBIN LANG. ALL RIGHTS RESERVED. NO PART OF THIS BOOK (EXCEPT SMALL PORTIONS FOR REVIEW PURPOSES) MAY BE REPRODUCED IN ANY FORM WITHOUT WRITTEN PERMISSION FROM DIANE OBOMSAWIN OR DRAWN & QUARTERLY. ORIGINALLY PUBLISHED IN FRENCH BY L'OIE DE CRAVAN.

DRAWNANDQUARTERLY.COM

FIRST PAPERBACK EDITION: FEBRUARY 2014. PRINTED IN CANADA. 10 9 8 7 6 5 4 3 2 1

LIBRARY AND ARCHIVES CANADA CATALOGUING IN PUBLICATION: OBOM, AUTHOR, ARTIST. ON LOVING WOMEN / DIANE OBOMSAWIN. ISBN 978-1-77046-140-6 (PBK.). 1. GRAPHIC NOVELS. I. TITLE. PN6734.05026 2013   741.5'971   C2013-902773-4

DRAWN & QUARTERLY AND DIANE OBOMSAWIN ACKNOWLEDGE THE FINANCIAL CONTRIBUTION OF THE GOVERNMENT OF CANADA THROUGH THE CANADA BOOK FUND AND THE CANADA COUNCIL FOR THE ARTS FOR OUR PUBLISHING ACTIVITIES AND FOR SUPPORT OF THIS EDITION.

PUBLISHED IN THE USA BY DRAWN & QUARTERLY, A CLIENT PUBLISHER OF FARRAR, STRAUS AND GIROUX. ORDERS: 888.330.8477

PUBLISHED IN CANADA BY DRAWN & QUARTERLY, A CLIENT PUBLISHER OF RAINCOAST BOOKS ORDERS: 800.663.5714

PUBLISHED IN THE UK BY DRAWN & QUARTERLY, A CLIENT PUBLISHER OF PUBLISHERS GROUP UK ORDERS: INFO@PGUK.CO.UK

ON LOVING WOMEN

DIANE OBOMSAWIN

TRANSLATED BY HELGE DASCHER

DRAWN & QUARTERLY

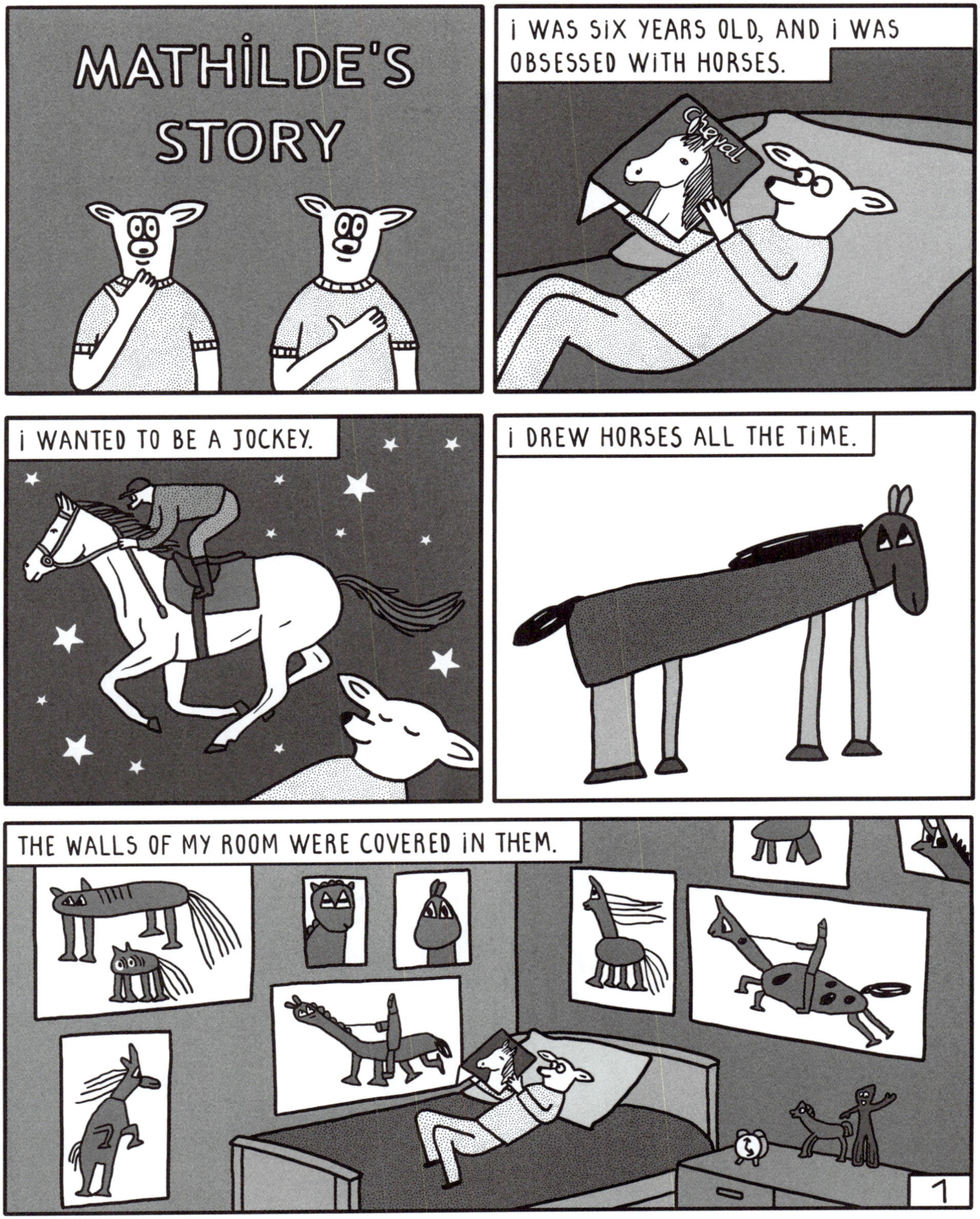
MATHiLDE'S STORY
i WAS SiX YEARS OLD, AND i WAS OBSESSED WiTH HORSES.
Cheval
i WANTED TO BE A JOCKEY.
i DREW HORSES ALL THE TiME.
THE WALLS OF MY ROOM WERE COVERED iN THEM.

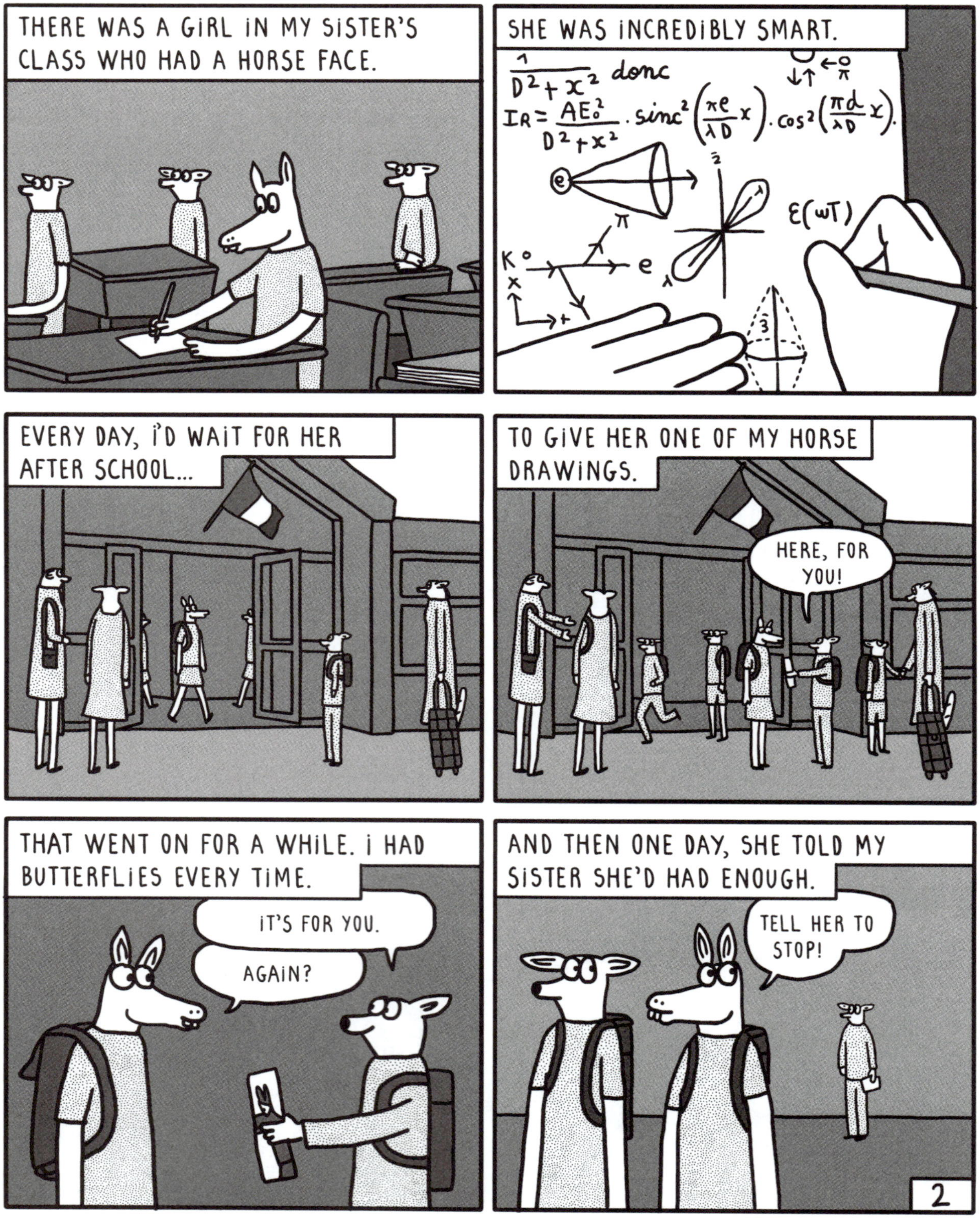
THERE WAS A GIRL IN MY SISTER'S CLASS WHO HAD A HORSE FACE.
SHE WAS INCREDIBLY SMART.
donc
EVERY DAY, I'D WAIT FOR HER AFTER SCHOOL...
TO GIVE HER ONE OF MY HORSE DRAWINGS.
HERE, FOR YOU!
THAT WENT ON FOR A WHILE. I HAD BUTTERFLIES EVERY TIME.
IT'S FOR YOU.
AGAIN?
AND THEN ONE DAY, SHE TOLD MY SISTER SHE'D HAD ENOUGH.
TELL HER TO STOP!

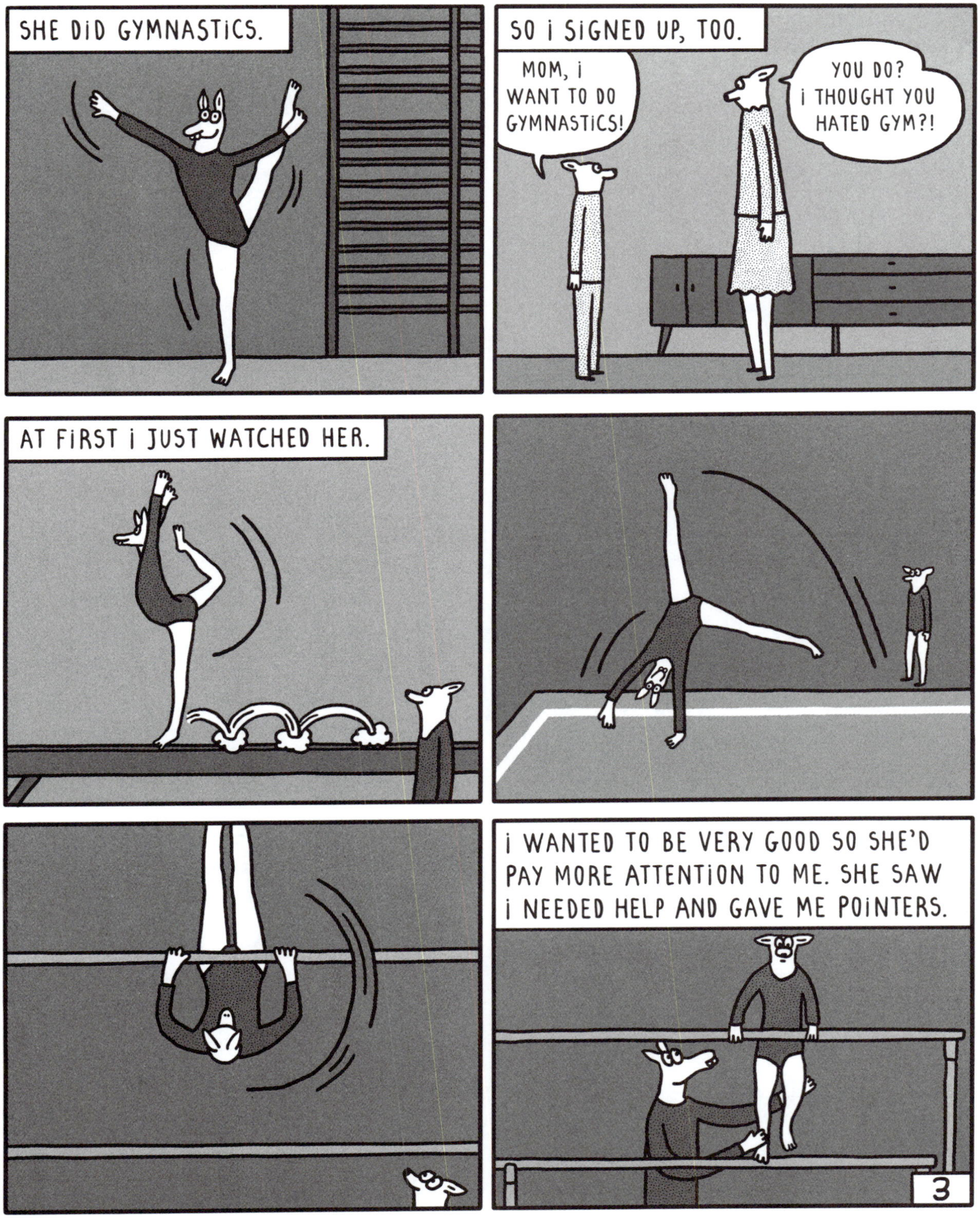
SHE DID GYMNASTICS.
SO I SIGNED UP, TOO.
MOM, I WANT TO DO GYMNASTICS!
YOU DO? I THOUGHT YOU HATED GYM?!
AT FIRST I JUST WATCHED HER.
I WANTED TO BE VERY GOOD SO SHE'D PAY MORE ATTENTION TO ME. SHE SAW I NEEDED HELP AND GAVE ME POINTERS.
3

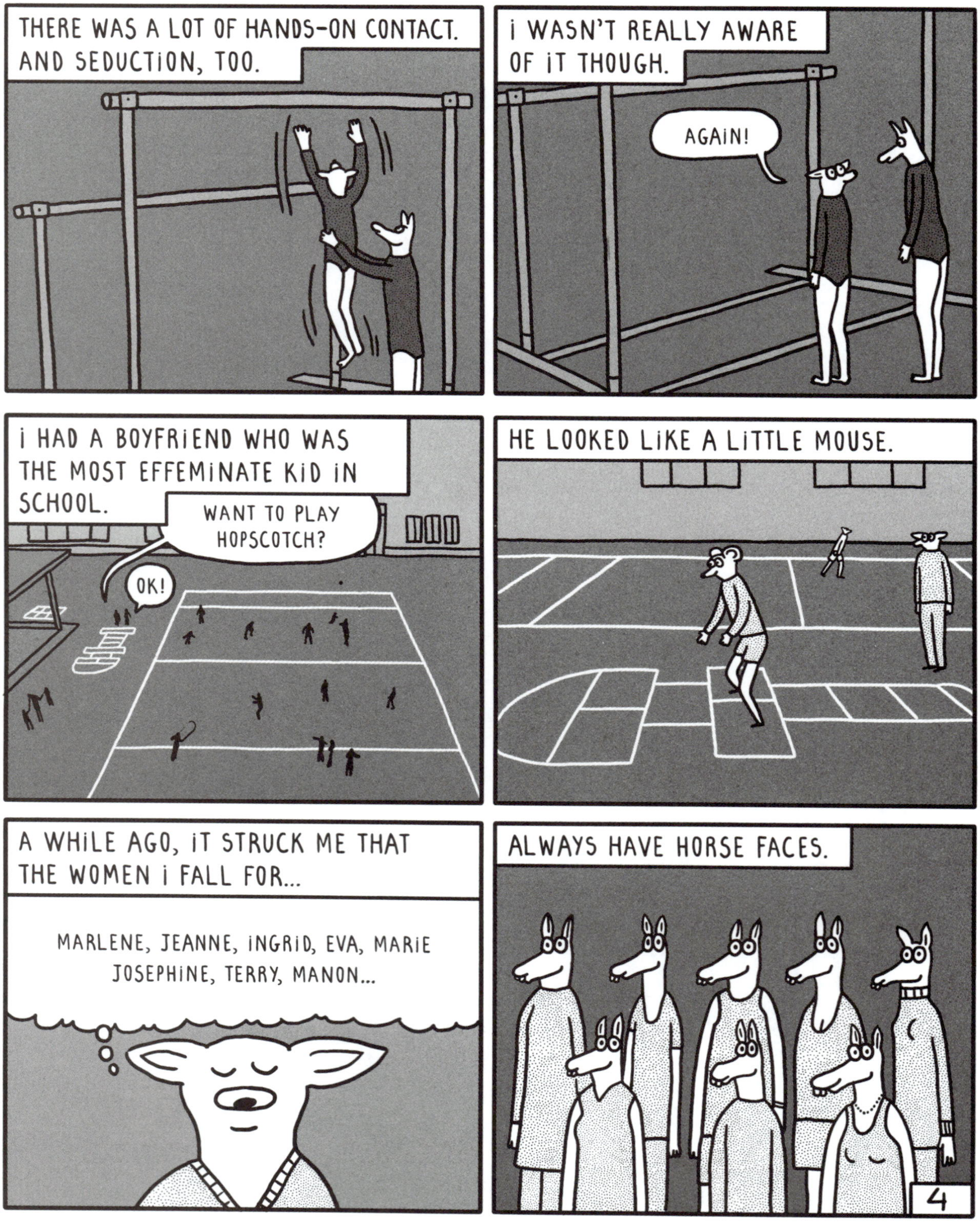
THERE WAS A LOT OF HANDS-ON CONTACT. AND SEDUCTION, TOO.
I WASN'T REALLY AWARE OF IT THOUGH.
AGAIN!
I HAD A BOYFRIEND WHO WAS THE MOST EFFEMINATE KID IN SCHOOL.
WANT TO PLAY HOPSCOTCH?
OK!
HE LOOKED LIKE A LITTLE MOUSE.
A WHILE AGO, IT STRUCK ME THAT THE WOMEN I FALL FOR...
MARLENE, JEANNE, INGRID, EVA, MARIE JOSEPHINE, TERRY, MANON...
ALWAYS HAVE HORSE FACES.
4

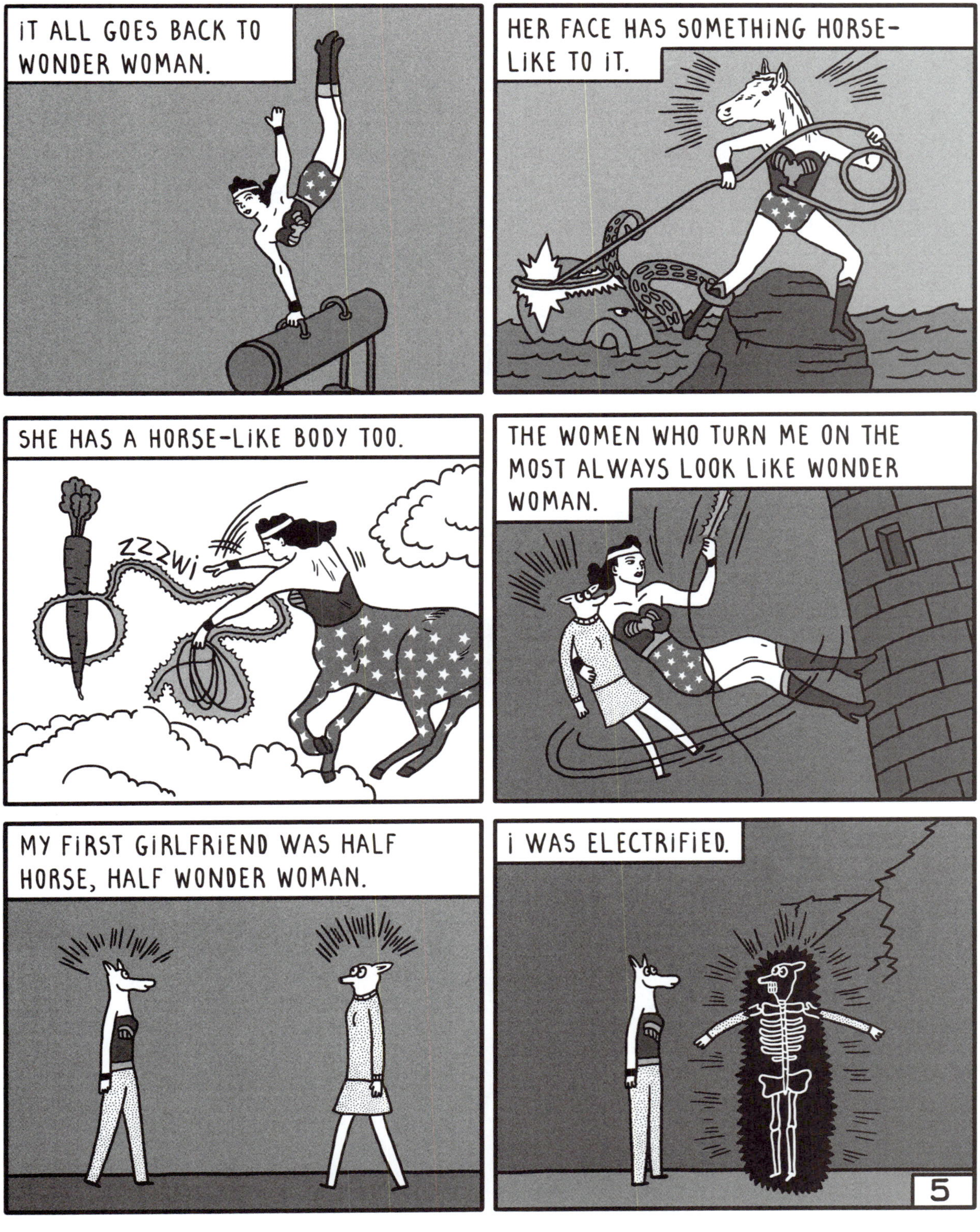

iT ALL GOES BACK TO WONDER WOMAN.
HER FACE HAS SOMETHiNG HORSE-LiKE TO iT.
SHE HAS A HORSE-LiKE BODY TOO.
ZZZWi
THE WOMEN WHO TURN ME ON THE MOST ALWAYS LOOK LiKE WONDER WOMAN.
MY FiRST GiRLFRiEND WAS HALF HORSE, HALF WONDER WOMAN.
i WAS ELECTRiFiED.

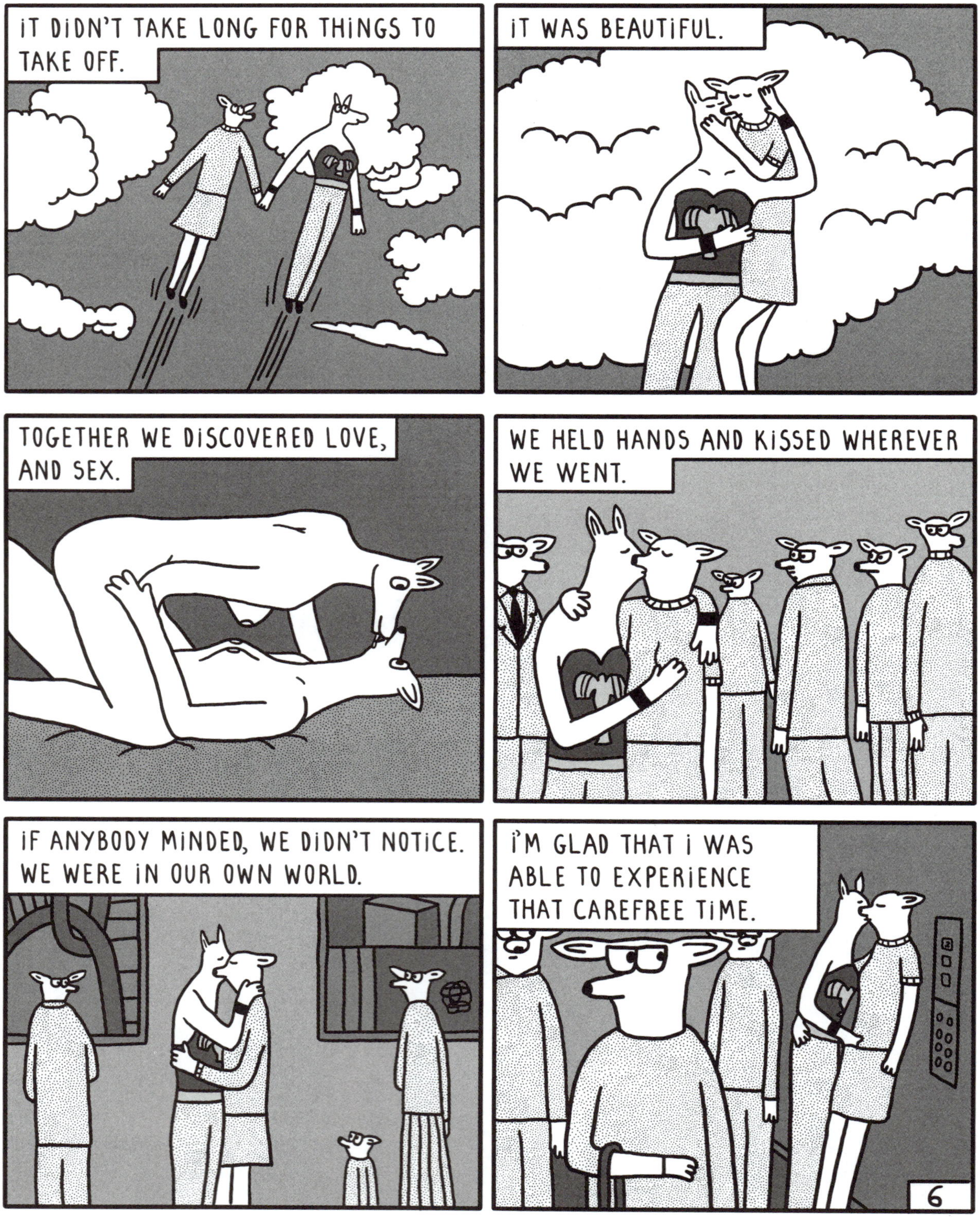
IT DIDN'T TAKE LONG FOR THINGS TO TAKE OFF.
IT WAS BEAUTIFUL.
TOGETHER WE DISCOVERED LOVE, AND SEX.
WE HELD HANDS AND KISSED WHEREVER WE WENT.
IF ANYBODY MINDED, WE DIDN'T NOTICE. WE WERE IN OUR OWN WORLD.
I'M GLAD THAT I WAS ABLE TO EXPERIENCE THAT CAREFREE TIME.

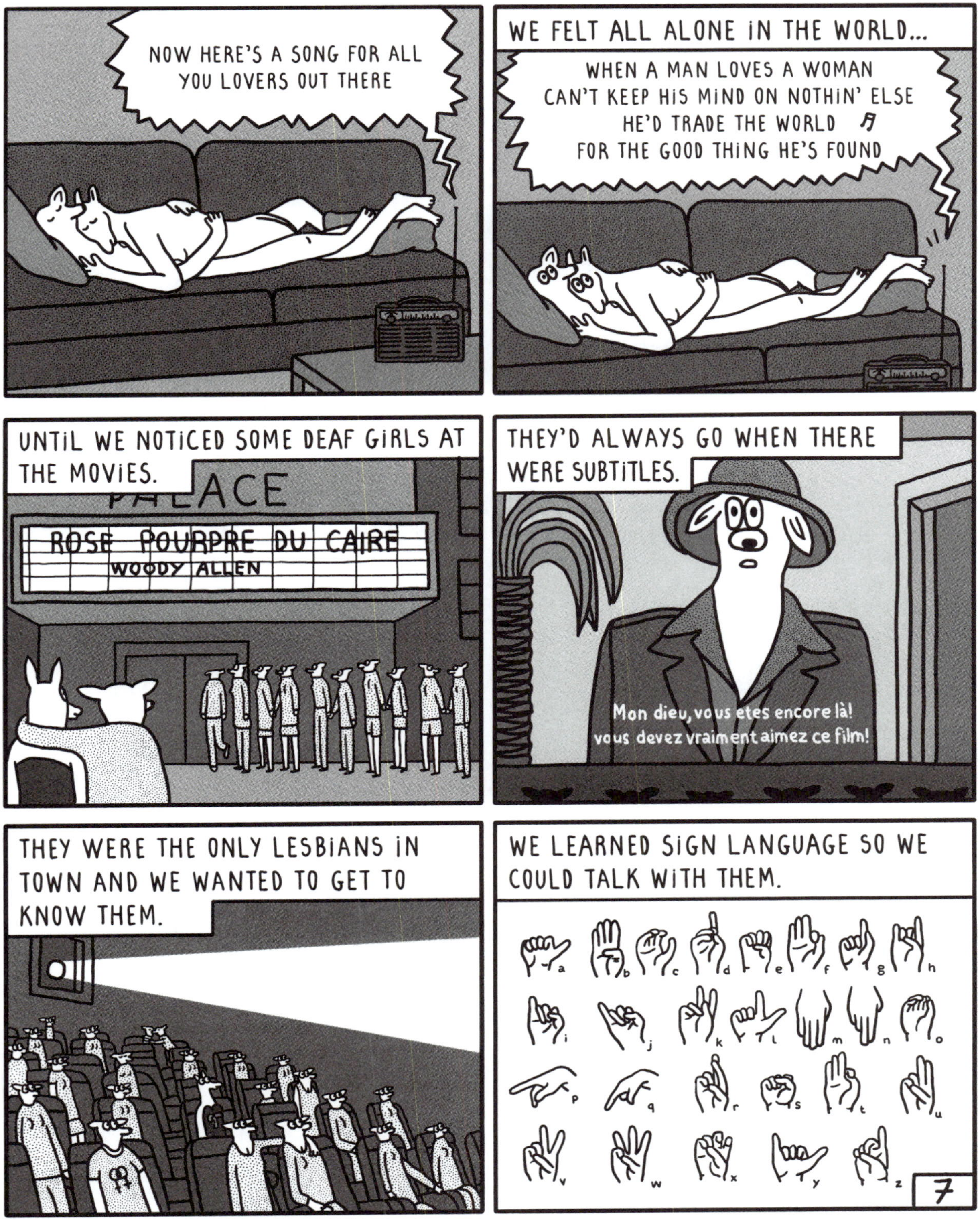
NOW HERE'S A SONG FOR ALL YOU LOVERS OUT THERE
WE FELT ALL ALONE IN THE WORLD...
WHEN A MAN LOVES A WOMAN
CAN'T KEEP HIS MIND ON NOTHIN' ELSE
HE'D TRADE THE WORLD
FOR THE GOOD THING HE'S FOUND
UNTIL WE NOTICED SOME DEAF GIRLS AT THE MOVIES.
PALACE
ROSE POURPRE DU CAIRE
WOODY ALLEN
THEY'D ALWAYS GO WHEN THERE WERE SUBTITLES.
Mon dieu, vous etes encore là!
vous devez vraiment aimez ce film!
THEY WERE THE ONLY LESBIANS IN TOWN AND WE WANTED TO GET TO KNOW THEM.
WE LEARNED SIGN LANGUAGE SO WE COULD TALK WITH THEM.
a b c d e f g h
i j k l m n o
p q r s t u
v w x y z

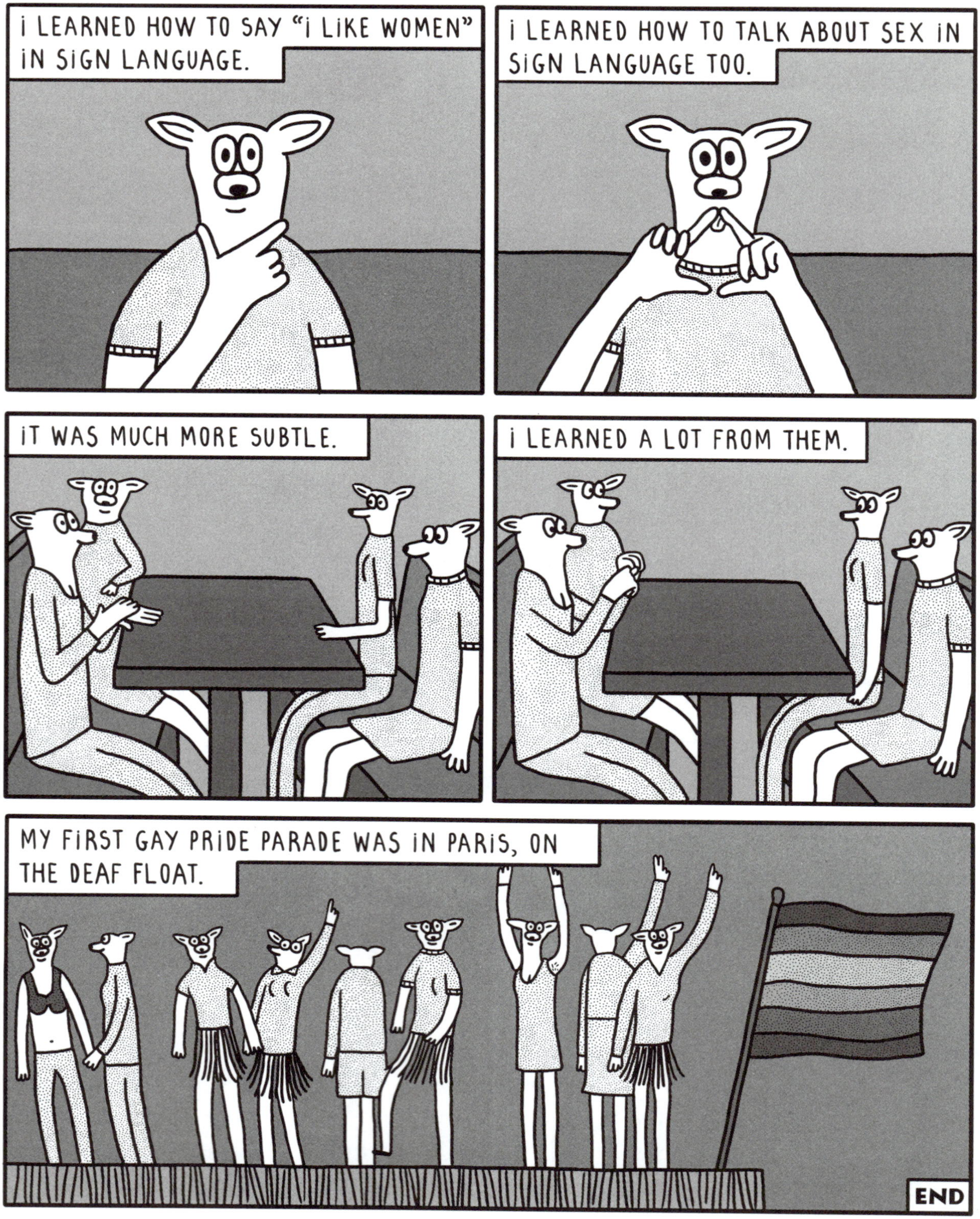
I LEARNED HOW TO SAY "I LIKE WOMEN" IN SIGN LANGUAGE.
I LEARNED HOW TO TALK ABOUT SEX IN SIGN LANGUAGE TOO.
IT WAS MUCH MORE SUBTLE.
I LEARNED A LOT FROM THEM.
MY FIRST GAY PRIDE PARADE WAS IN PARIS, ON THE DEAF FLOAT.
END

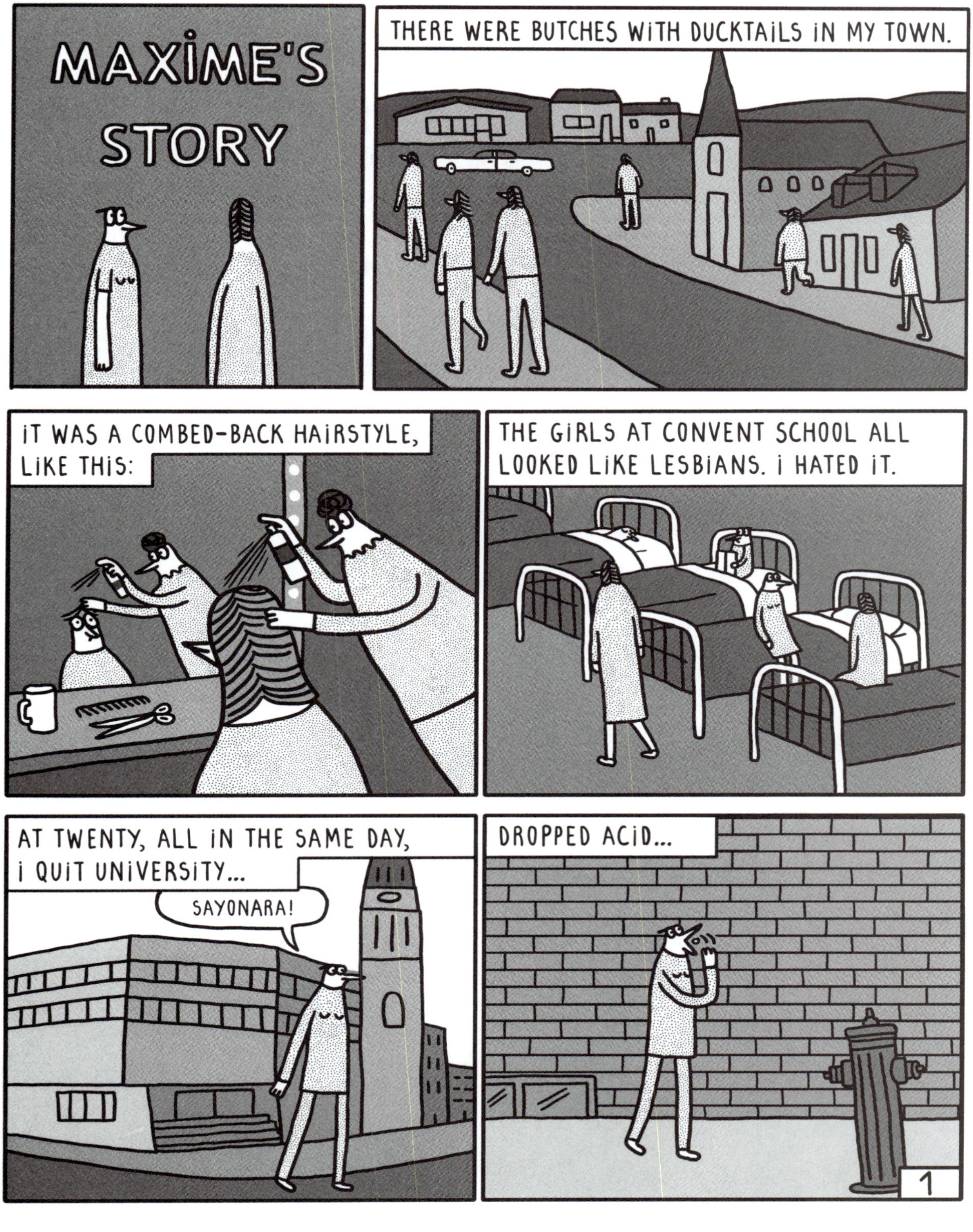
MAXIME'S STORY
THERE WERE BUTCHES WITH DUCKTAILS IN MY TOWN.
IT WAS A COMBED-BACK HAIRSTYLE, LIKE THIS:
THE GIRLS AT CONVENT SCHOOL ALL LOOKED LIKE LESBIANS. I HATED IT.
AT TWENTY, ALL IN THE SAME DAY, I QUIT UNIVERSITY...
SAYONARA!
DROPPED ACID...

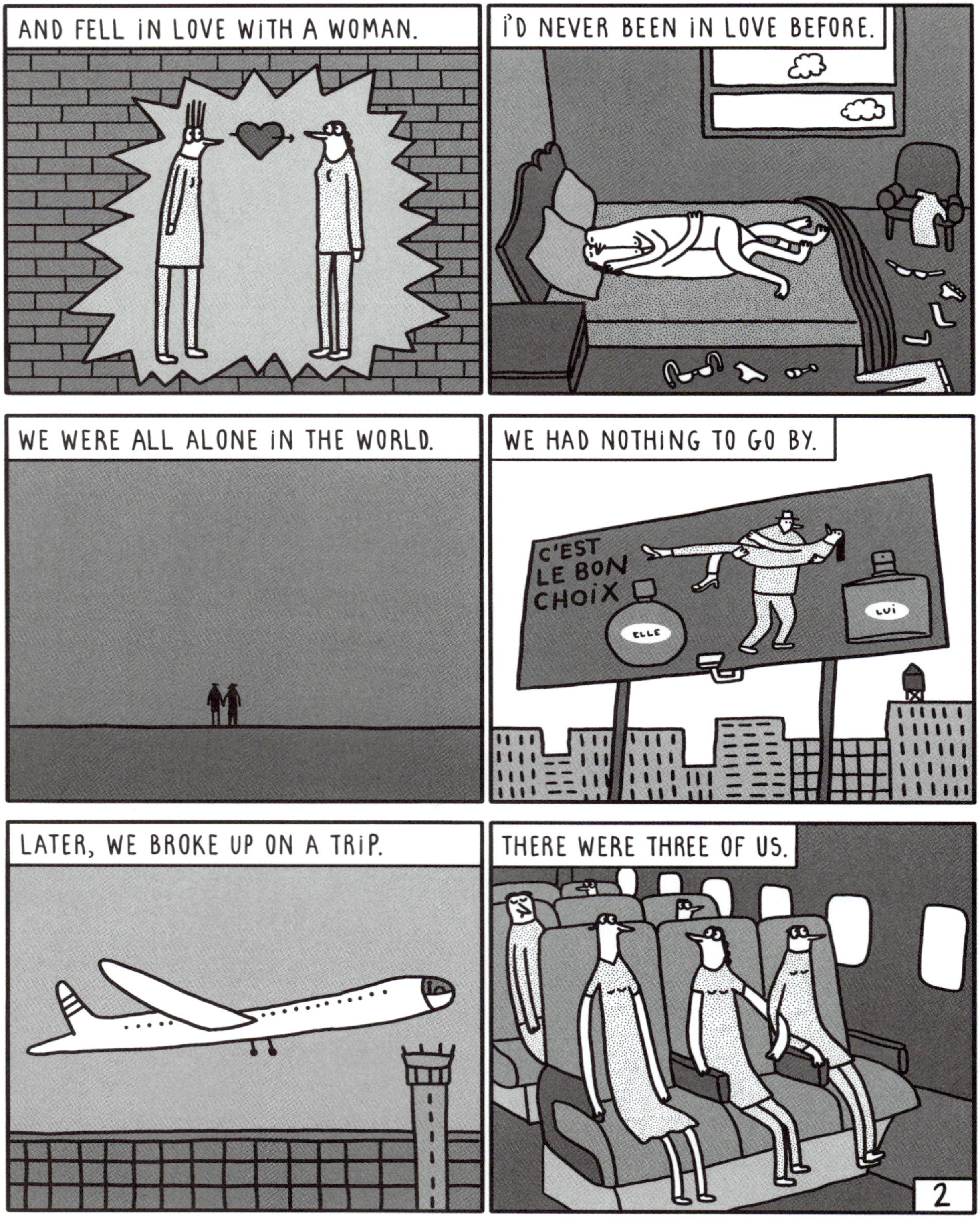
AND FELL IN LOVE WITH A WOMAN.
I'D NEVER BEEN IN LOVE BEFORE.
WE WERE ALL ALONE IN THE WORLD.
WE HAD NOTHING TO GO BY.
C'EST LE BON CHOIX
ELLE
LUI
LATER, WE BROKE UP ON A TRIP.
THERE WERE THREE OF US.

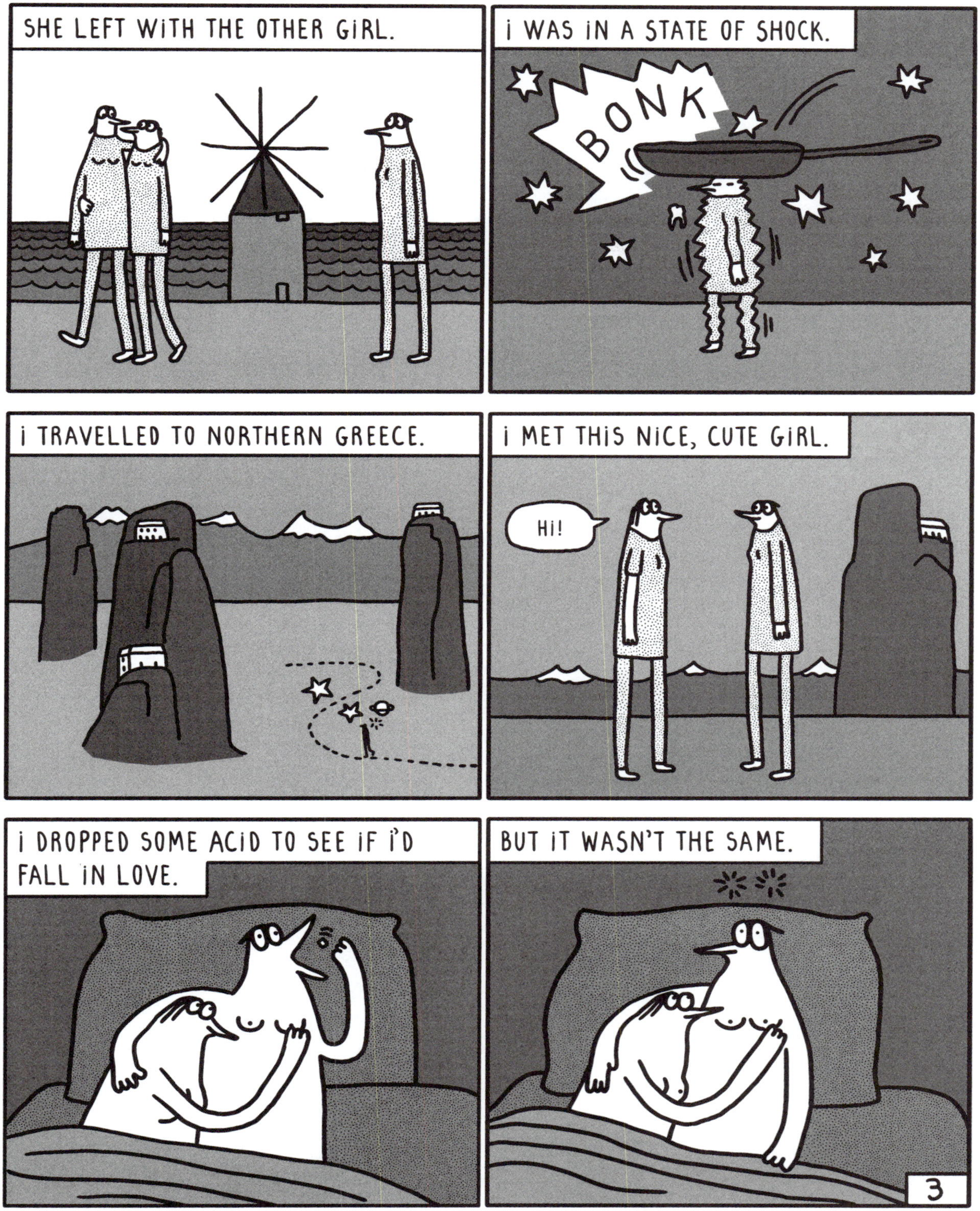
SHE LEFT WiTH THE OTHER GiRL.
i WAS iN A STATE OF SHOCK.
BONK
i TRAVELLED TO NORTHERN GREECE.
i MET THiS NiCE, CUTE GiRL.
Hi!
i DROPPED SOME ACiD TO SEE iF i'D FALL iN LOVE.
BUT iT WASN'T THE SAME.

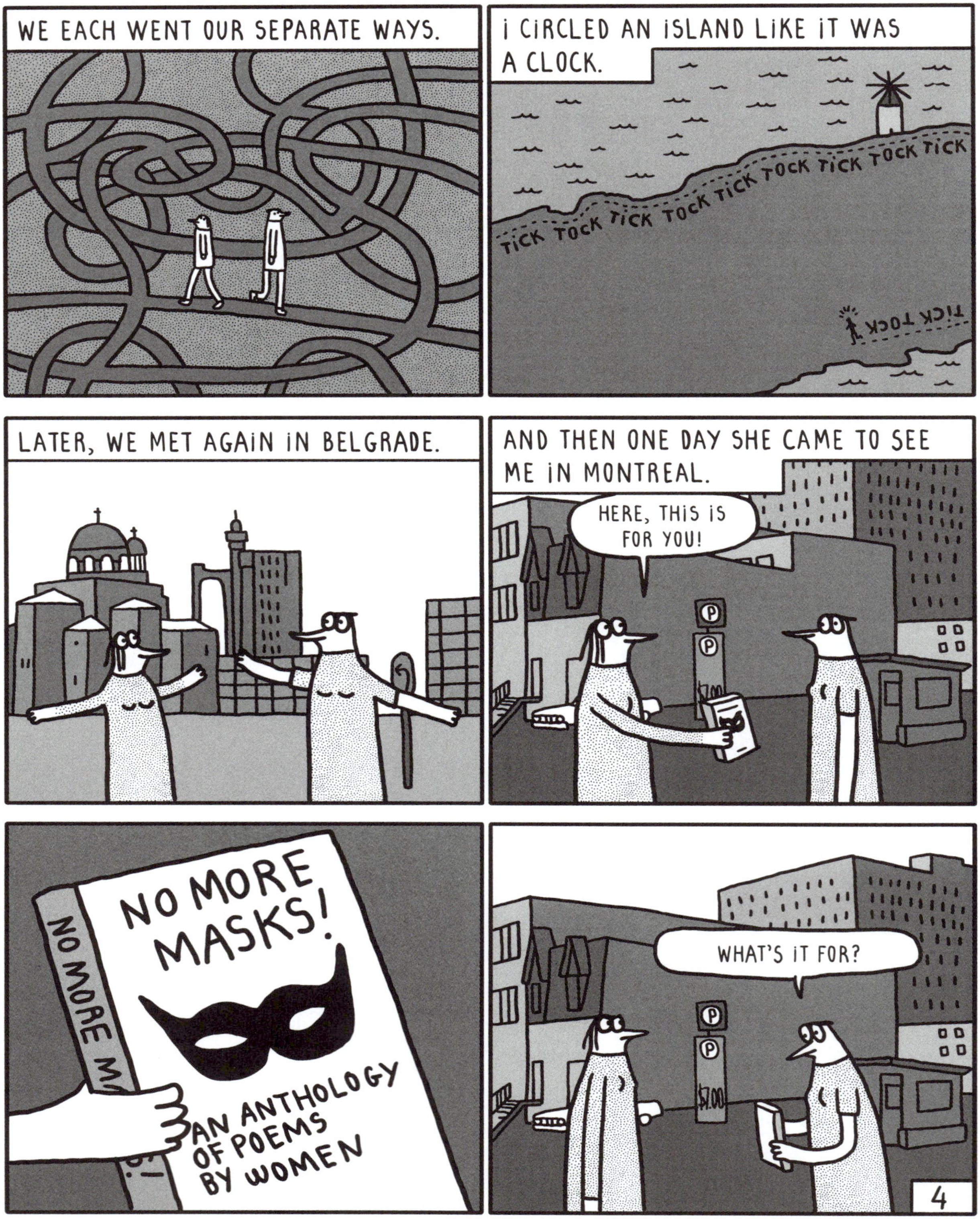
WE EACH WENT OUR SEPARATE WAYS.
I CIRCLED AN ISLAND LIKE IT WAS A CLOCK.
TICK TOCK TICK TOCK TICK TOCK TICK TOCK TICK
TICK TOCK
LATER, WE MET AGAIN IN BELGRADE.
AND THEN ONE DAY SHE CAME TO SEE ME IN MONTREAL.
HERE, THIS IS FOR YOU!
NO MORE MASKS!
AN ANTHOLOGY OF POEMS BY WOMEN
NO MORE M
WHAT'S IT FOR?
$7.00

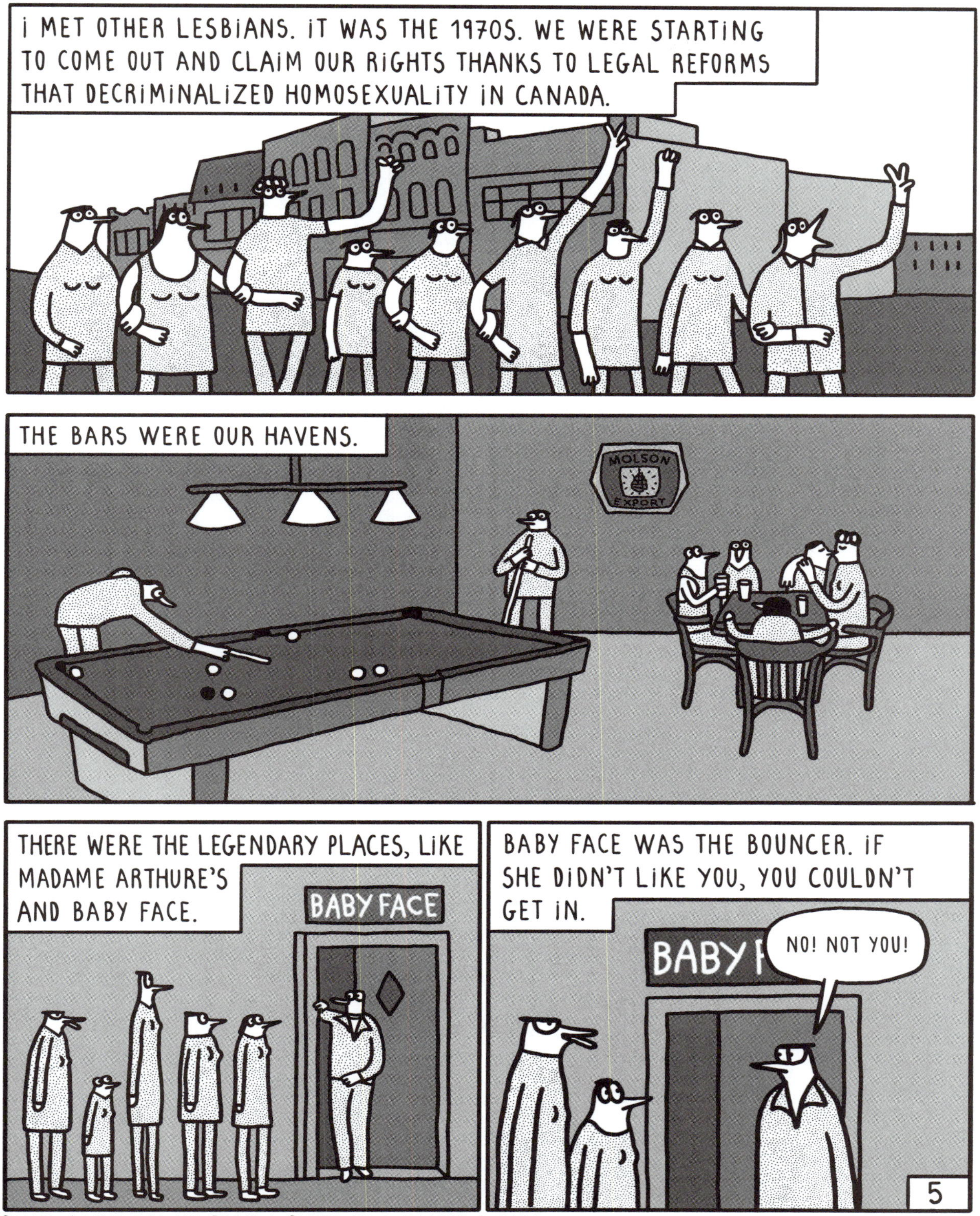
I MET OTHER LESBIANS. IT WAS THE 1970S. WE WERE STARTING TO COME OUT AND CLAIM OUR RIGHTS THANKS TO LEGAL REFORMS THAT DECRIMINALIZED HOMOSEXUALITY IN CANADA.
THE BARS WERE OUR HAVENS.
MOLSON EXPORT
THERE WERE THE LEGENDARY PLACES, LIKE MADAME ARTHURE'S AND BABY FACE.
BABY FACE
BABY FACE WAS THE BOUNCER. IF SHE DIDN'T LIKE YOU, YOU COULDN'T GET IN.
NO! NOT YOU!
PANEL ABOVE DRAWN FROM A PHOTO BY SUZANNE GIRARD.

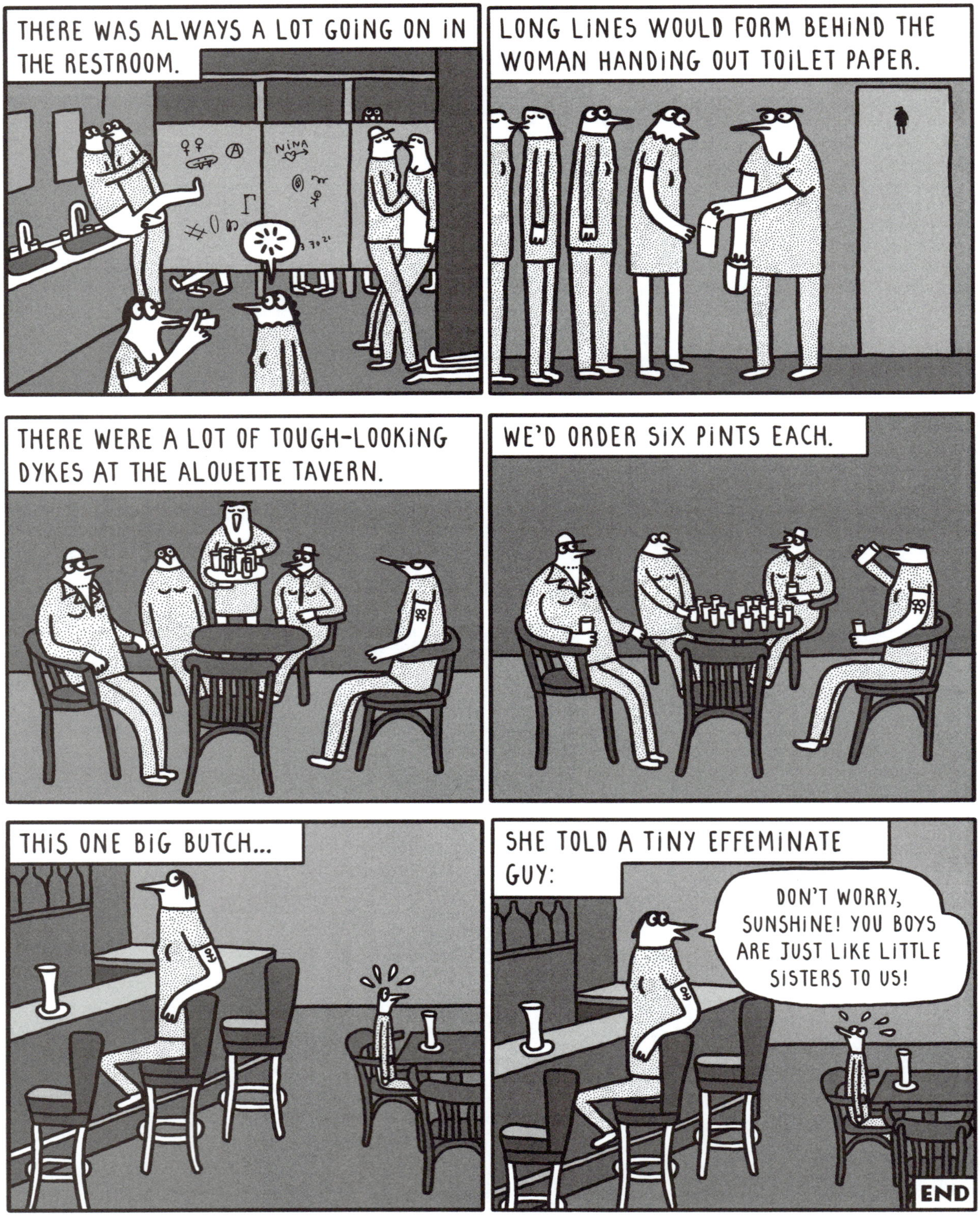
THERE WAS ALWAYS A LOT GOING ON IN THE RESTROOM.
NINA
LONG LINES WOULD FORM BEHIND THE WOMAN HANDING OUT TOILET PAPER.
THERE WERE A LOT OF TOUGH-LOOKING DYKES AT THE ALOUETTE TAVERN.
WE'D ORDER SIX PINTS EACH.
THIS ONE BIG BUTCH...
SHE TOLD A TINY EFFEMINATE GUY:
DON'T WORRY, SUNSHINE! YOU BOYS ARE JUST LIKE LITTLE SISTERS TO US!
END

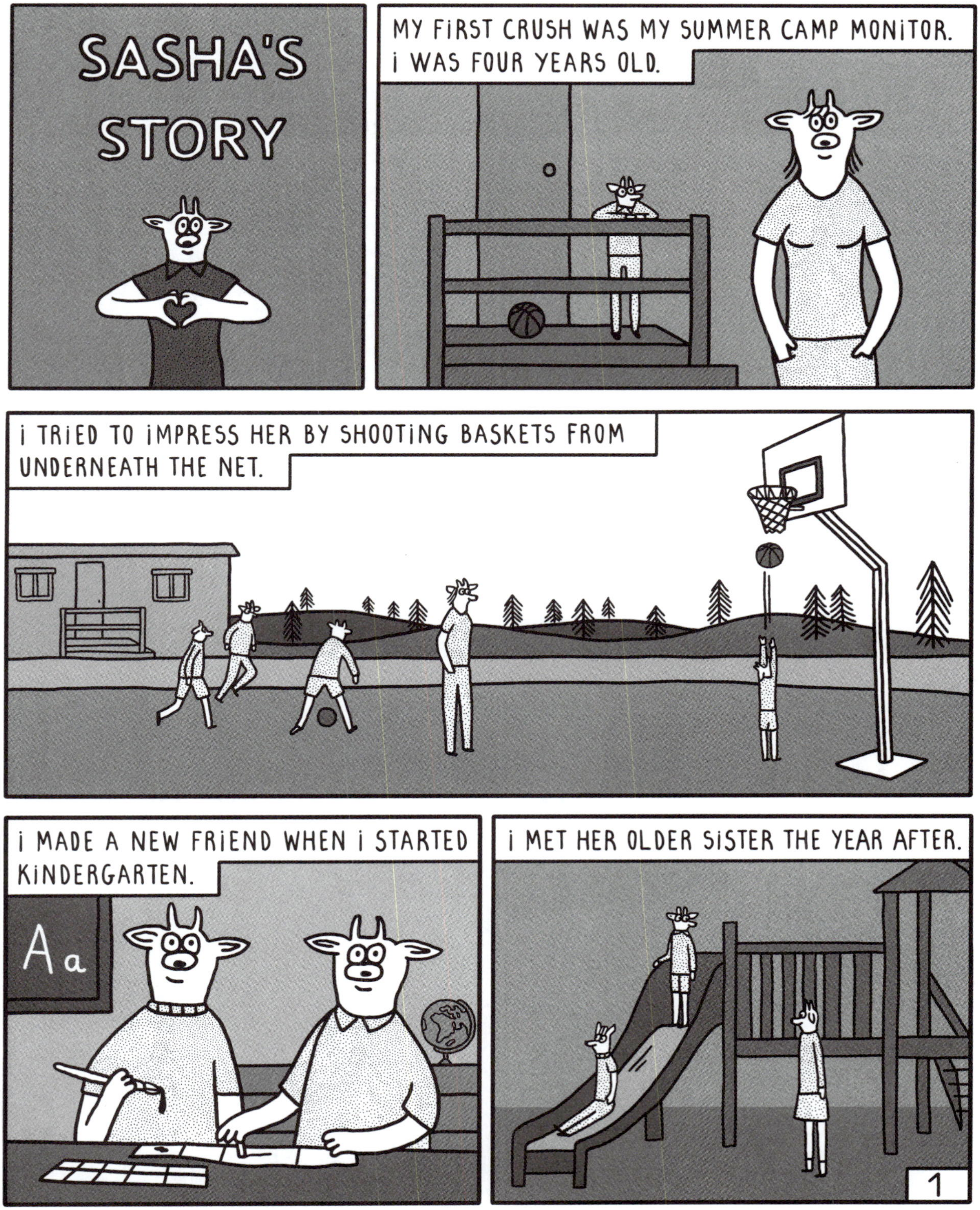
SASHA'S STORY
MY FIRST CRUSH WAS MY SUMMER CAMP MONITOR. I WAS FOUR YEARS OLD.
I TRIED TO IMPRESS HER BY SHOOTING BASKETS FROM UNDERNEATH THE NET.
I MADE A NEW FRIEND WHEN I STARTED KINDERGARTEN.
Aa
I MET HER OLDER SISTER THE YEAR AFTER.

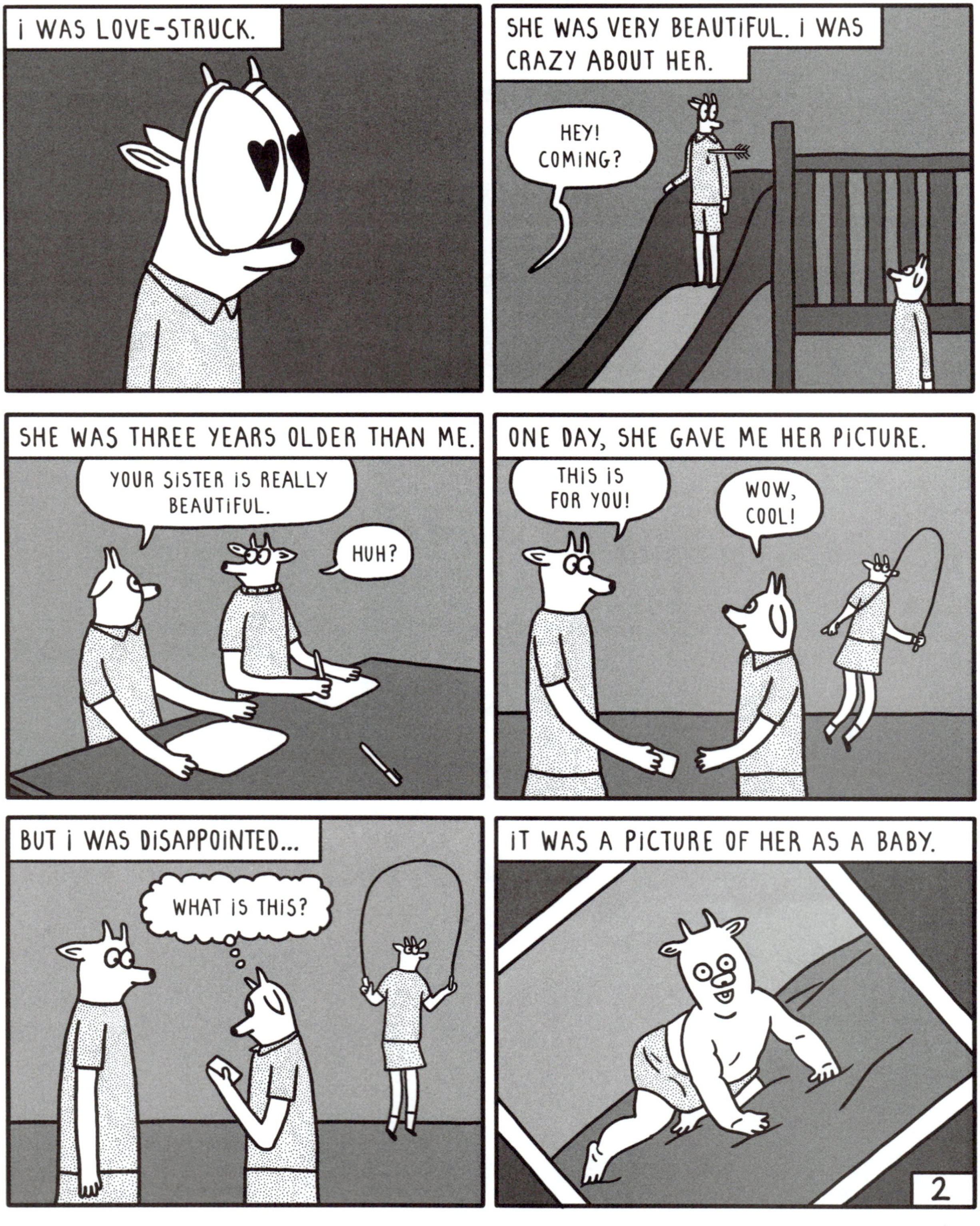
i WAS LOVE-STRUCK.
SHE WAS VERY BEAUTiFUL. i WAS CRAZY ABOUT HER.
HEY! COMiNG?
SHE WAS THREE YEARS OLDER THAN ME.
YOUR SiSTER iS REALLY BEAUTiFUL.
HUH?
ONE DAY, SHE GAVE ME HER PiCTURE.
THiS iS FOR YOU!
WOW, COOL!
BUT i WAS DiSAPPOiNTED...
WHAT iS THiS?
iT WAS A PiCTURE OF HER AS A BABY.

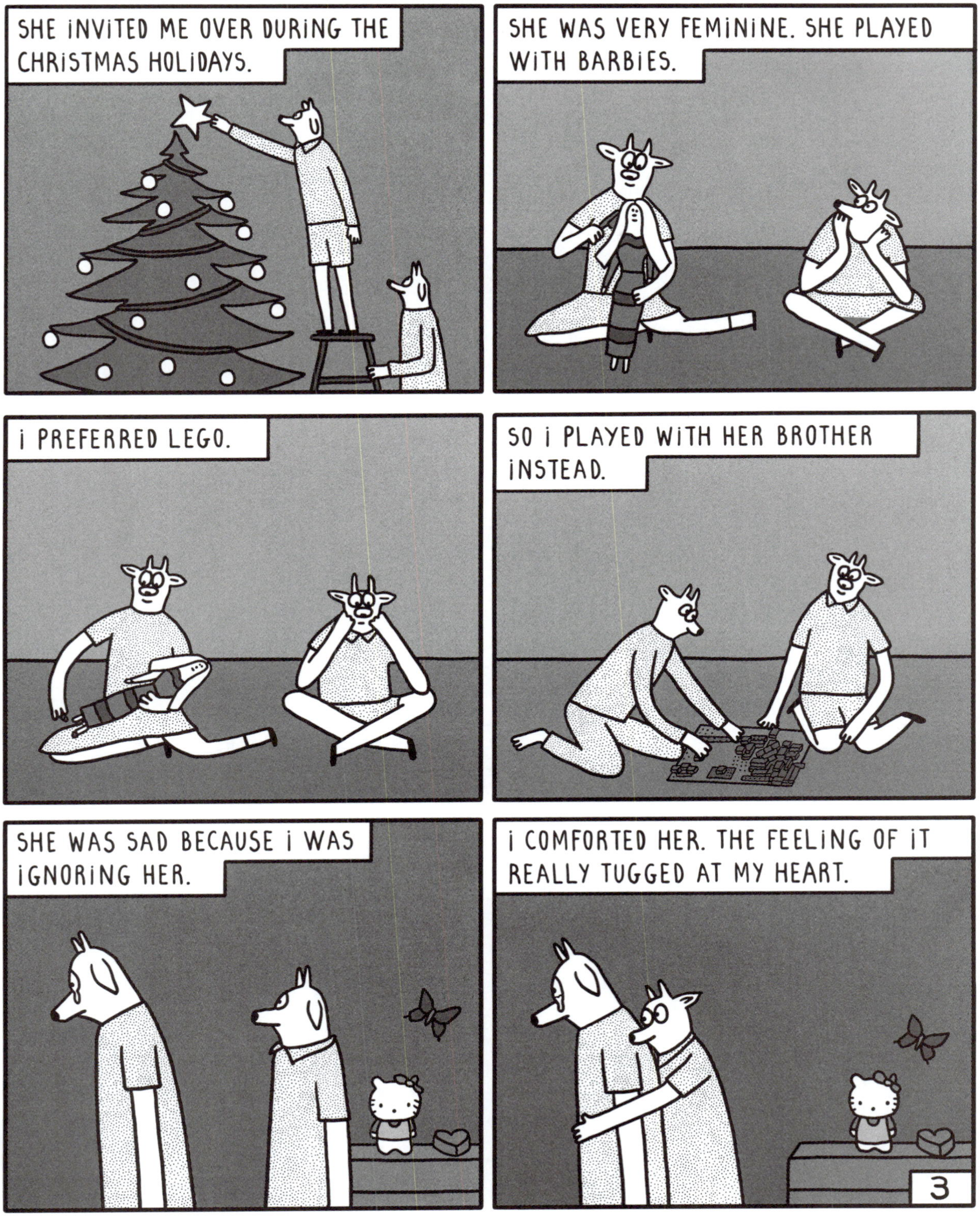
SHE INVITED ME OVER DURING THE CHRISTMAS HOLIDAYS.
SHE WAS VERY FEMININE. SHE PLAYED WITH BARBIES.
I PREFERRED LEGO.
SO I PLAYED WITH HER BROTHER INSTEAD.
SHE WAS SAD BECAUSE I WAS IGNORING HER.
I COMFORTED HER. THE FEELING OF IT REALLY TUGGED AT MY HEART.

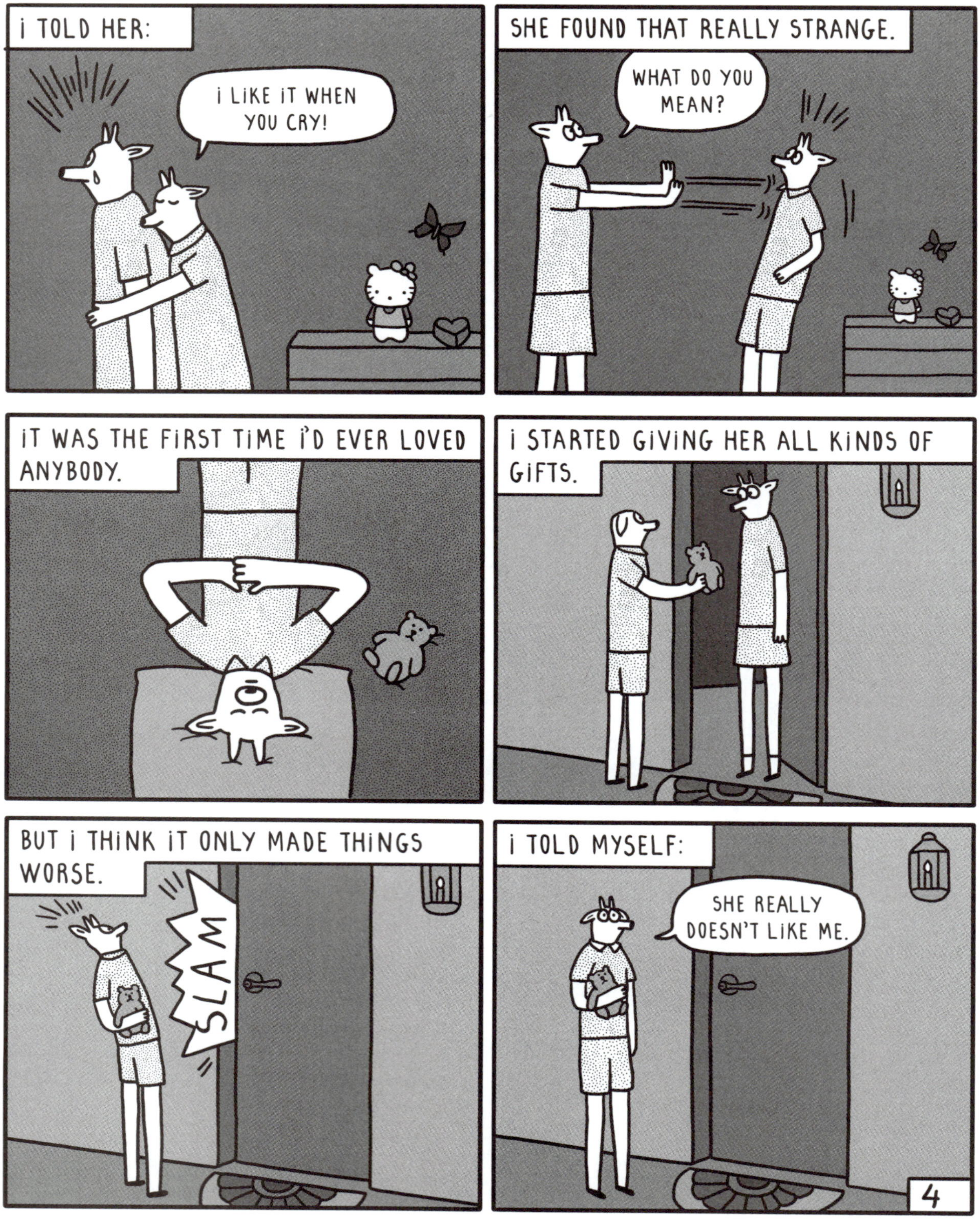
i TOLD HER:
i LIKE iT WHEN YOU CRY!
SHE FOUND THAT REALLY STRANGE.
WHAT DO YOU MEAN?
iT WAS THE FiRST TiME i'D EVER LOVED ANYBODY.
i STARTED GiViNG HER ALL KiNDS OF GiFTS.
BUT i THiNK iT ONLY MADE THiNGS WORSE.
SLAM
i TOLD MYSELF:
SHE REALLY DOESN'T LiKE ME.

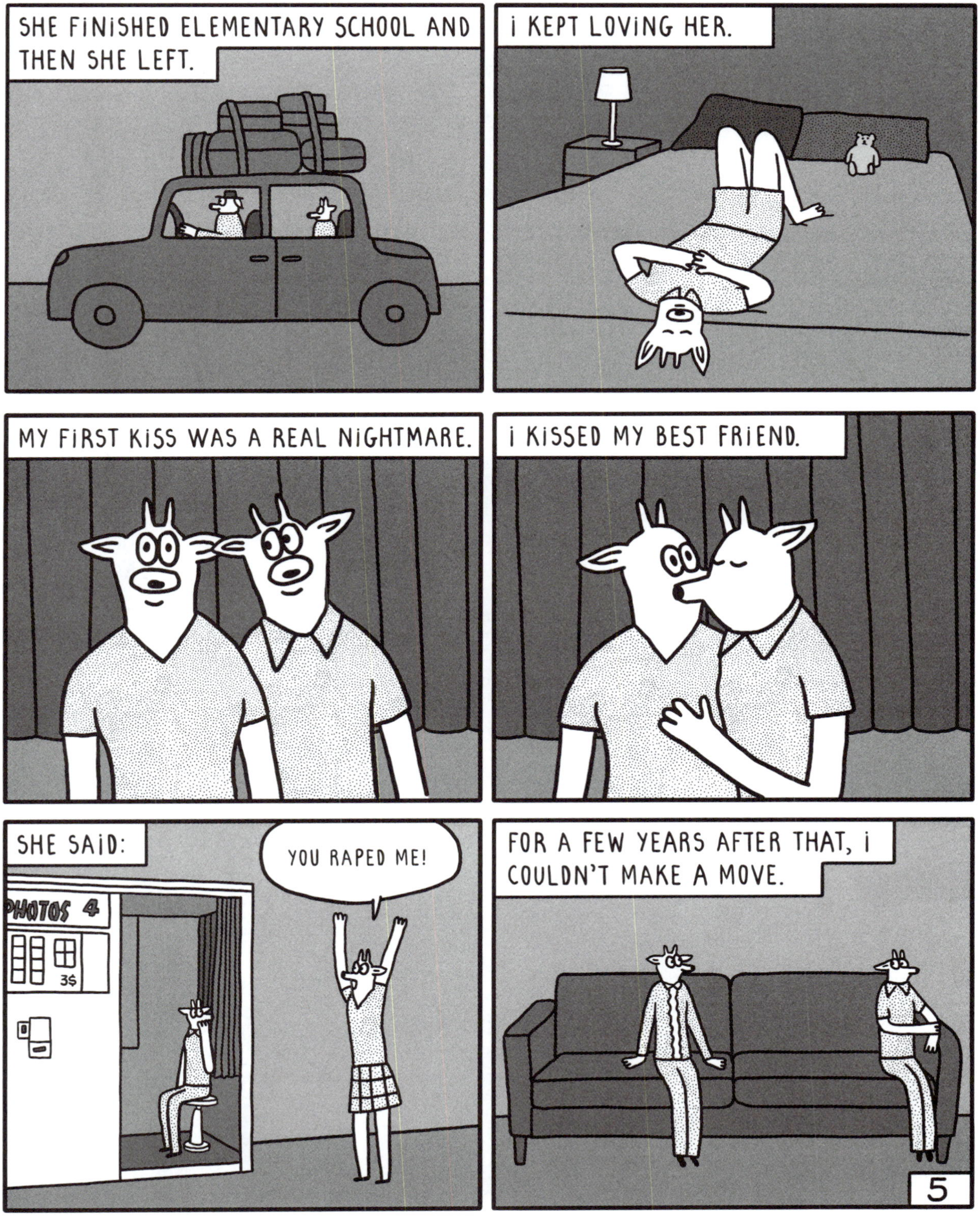
SHE FINISHED ELEMENTARY SCHOOL AND THEN SHE LEFT.
I KEPT LOVING HER.
MY FIRST KISS WAS A REAL NIGHTMARE.
I KISSED MY BEST FRIEND.
SHE SAID:
YOU RAPED ME!
PHOTOS 4
3$
FOR A FEW YEARS AFTER THAT, I COULDN'T MAKE A MOVE.

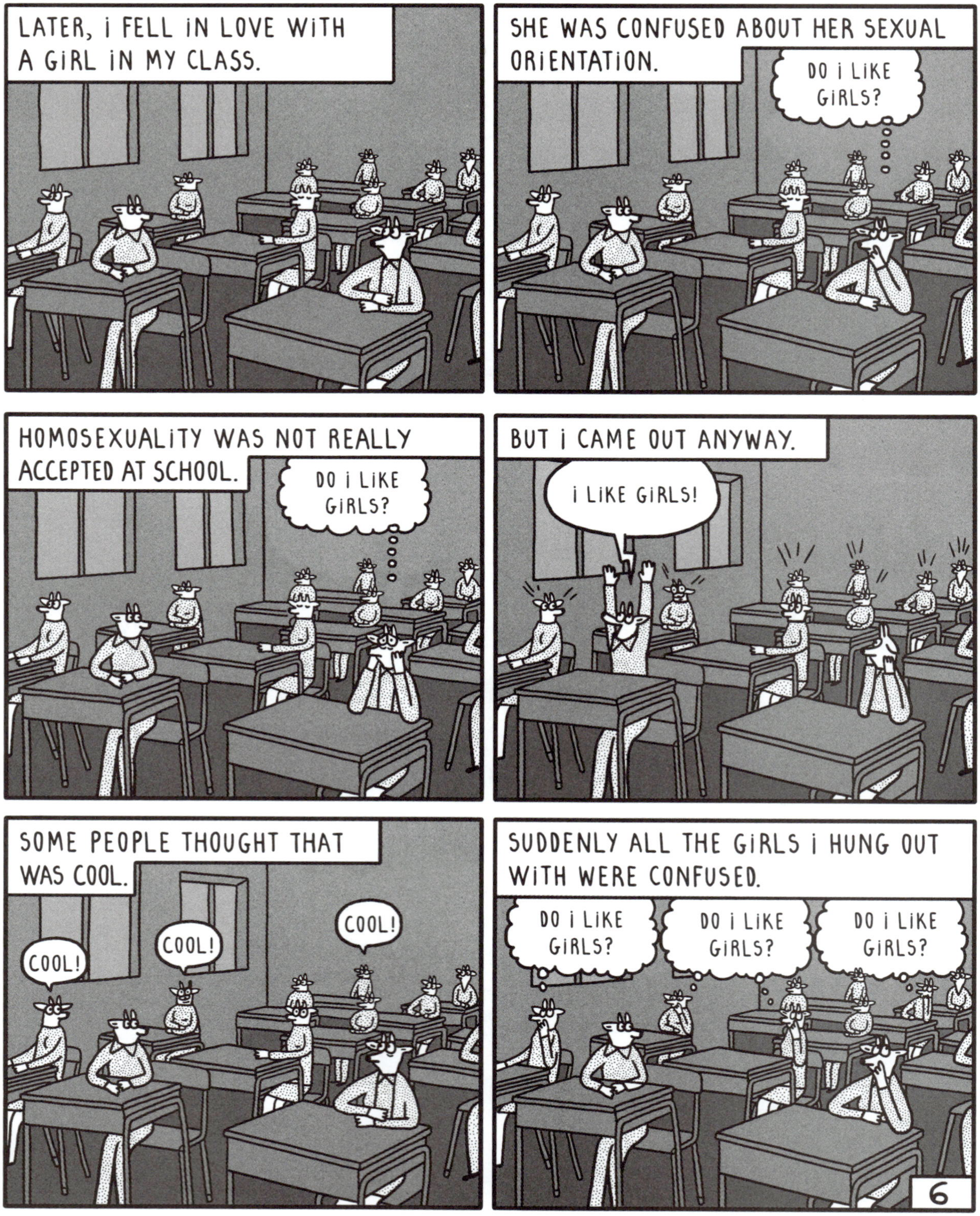
LATER, i FELL iN LOVE WiTH A GiRL iN MY CLASS.
SHE WAS CONFUSED ABOUT HER SEXUAL ORiENTATiON.
DO i LiKE GiRLS?
HOMOSEXUALiTY WAS NOT REALLY ACCEPTED AT SCHOOL.
DO i LiKE GiRLS?
BUT i CAME OUT ANYWAY.
i LiKE GiRLS!
SOME PEOPLE THOUGHT THAT WAS COOL.
COOL!
COOL!
COOL!
SUDDENLY ALL THE GiRLS i HUNG OUT WiTH WERE CONFUSED.
DO i LiKE GiRLS?
DO i LiKE GiRLS?
DO i LiKE GiRLS?
6

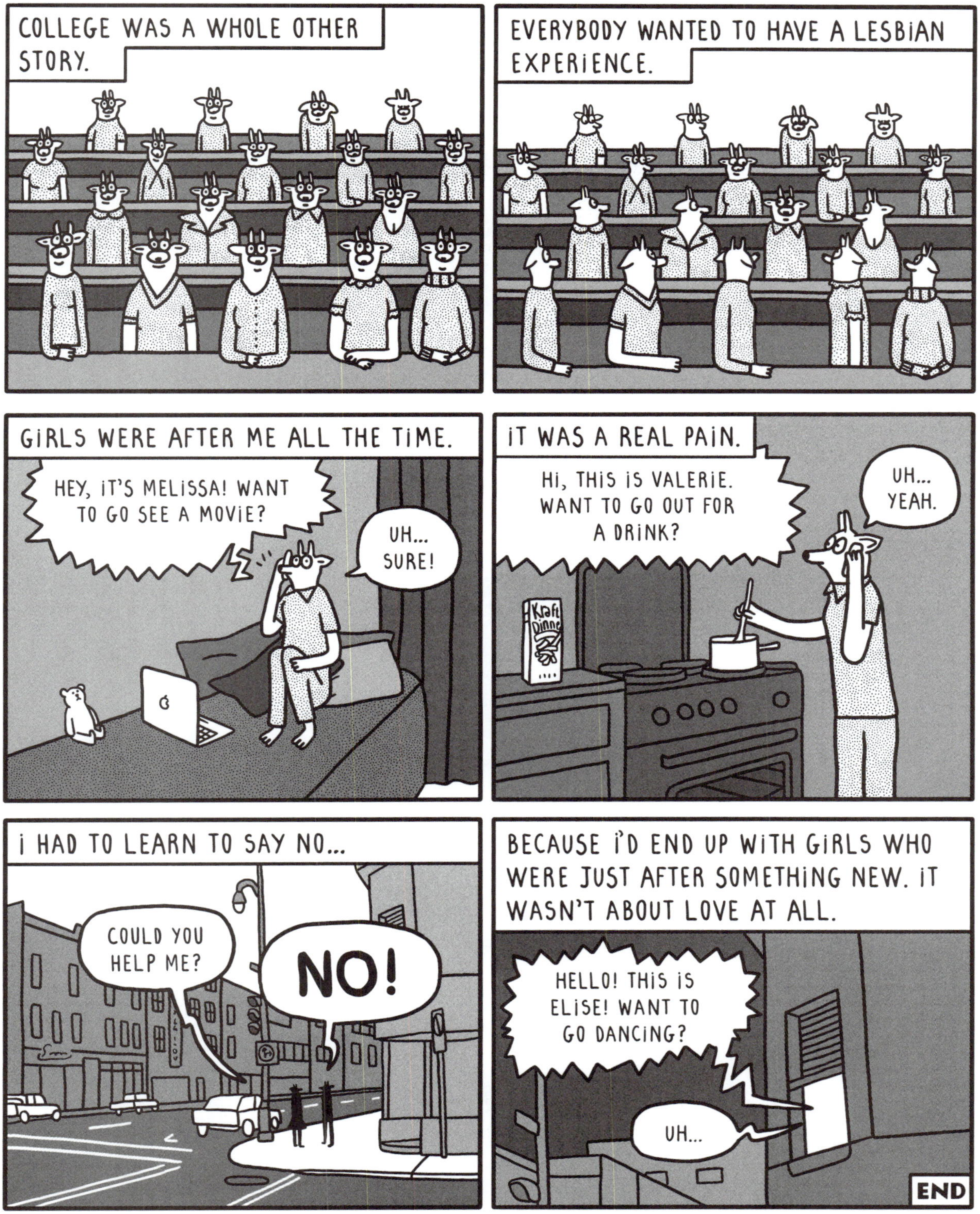
COLLEGE WAS A WHOLE OTHER STORY.
EVERYBODY WANTED TO HAVE A LESBIAN EXPERIENCE.
GIRLS WERE AFTER ME ALL THE TIME.
HEY, IT'S MELISSA! WANT TO GO SEE A MOVIE?
UH... SURE!
IT WAS A REAL PAIN.
HI, THIS IS VALERIE. WANT TO GO OUT FOR A DRINK?
UH... YEAH.
Kraft Dinner
I HAD TO LEARN TO SAY NO...
COULD YOU HELP ME?
NO!
BECAUSE I'D END UP WITH GIRLS WHO WERE JUST AFTER SOMETHING NEW. IT WASN'T ABOUT LOVE AT ALL.
HELLO! THIS IS ELISE! WANT TO GO DANCING?
UH...
END

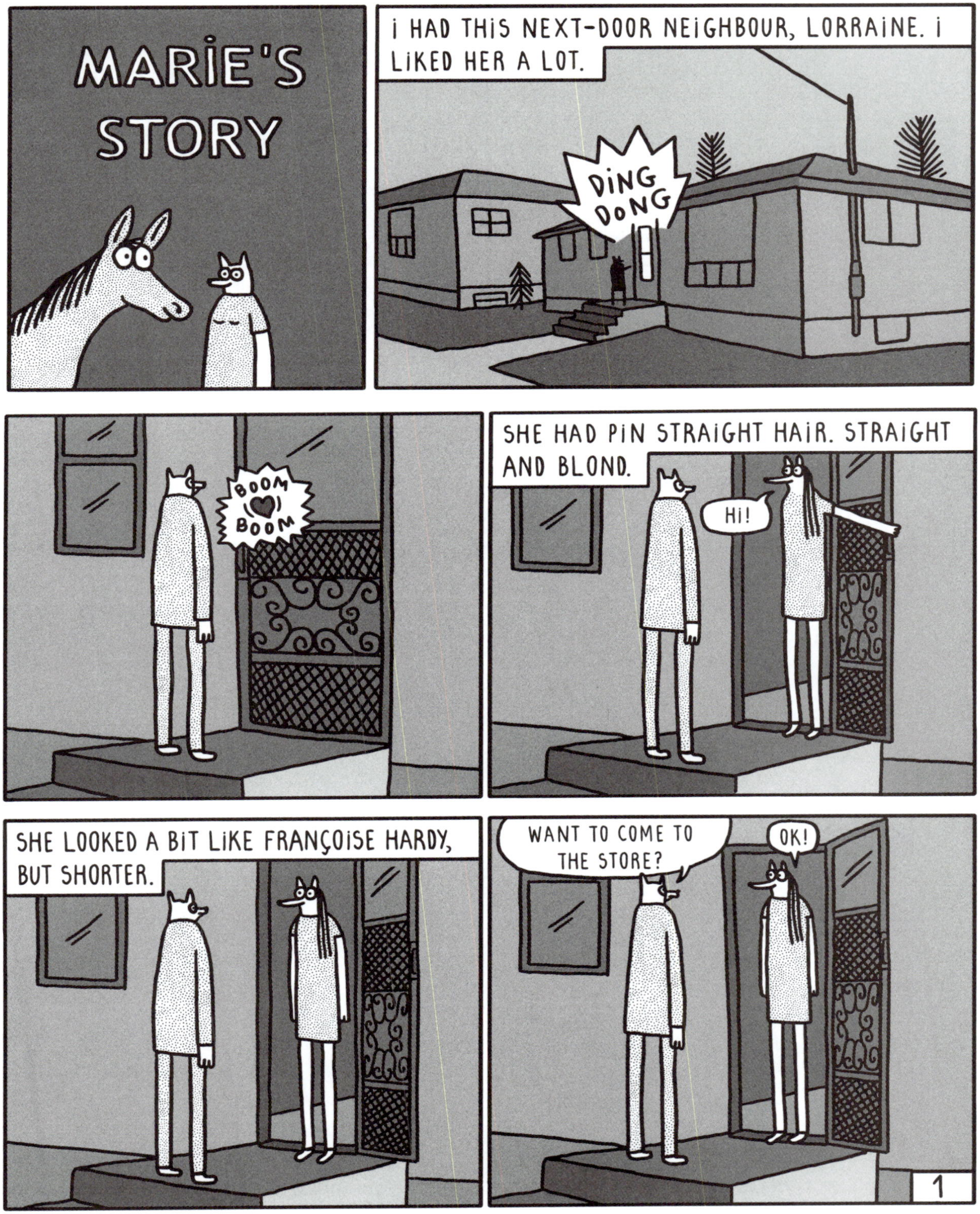
MARIE'S STORY
I HAD THIS NEXT-DOOR NEIGHBOUR, LORRAINE. I LIKED HER A LOT.
DING DONG
BOOM BOOM
SHE HAD PIN STRAIGHT HAIR. STRAIGHT AND BLOND.
HI!
SHE LOOKED A BIT LIKE FRANÇOISE HARDY, BUT SHORTER.
WANT TO COME TO THE STORE?
OK!

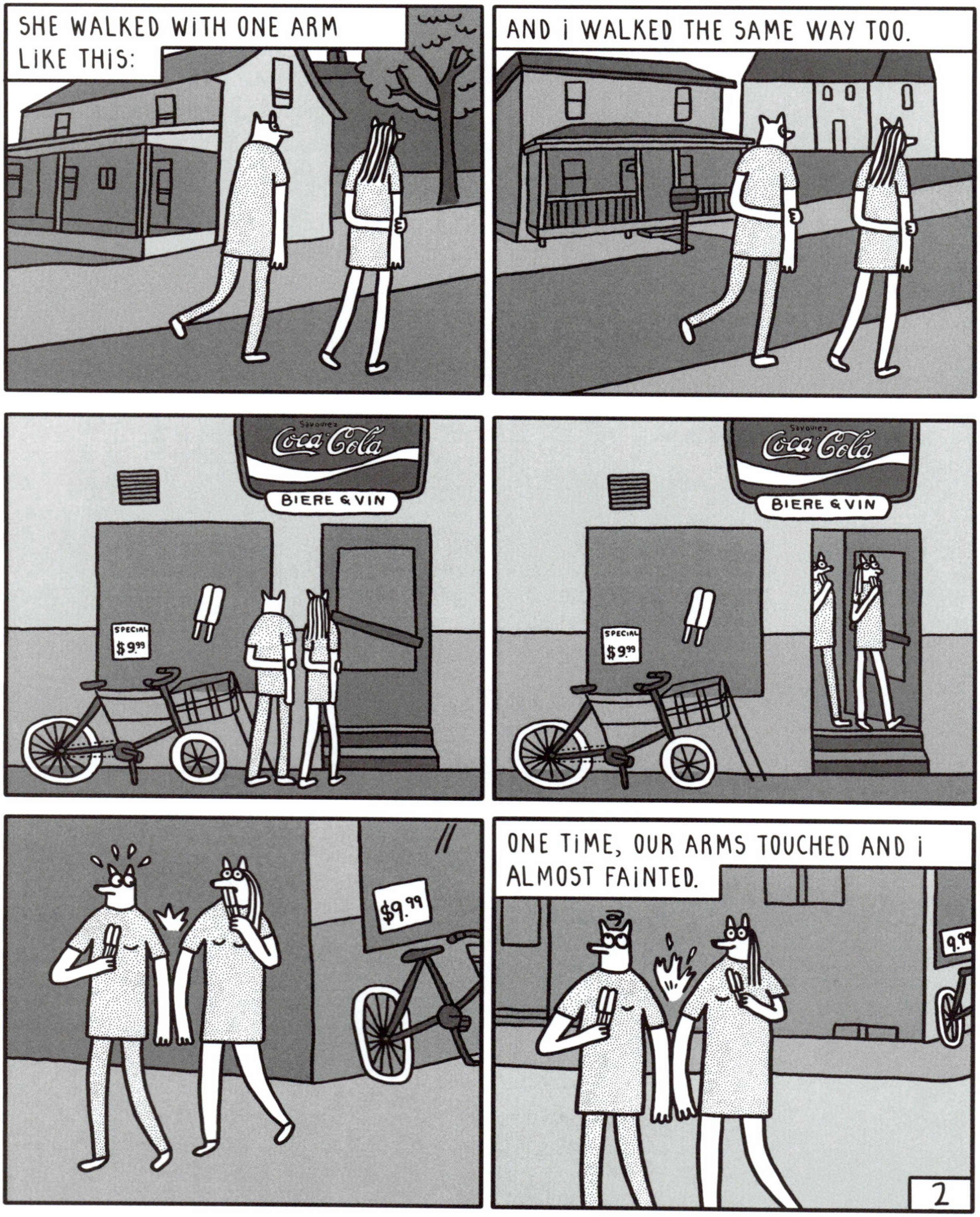
SHE WALKED WITH ONE ARM LIKE THIS:
AND I WALKED THE SAME WAY TOO.
Coca-Cola
BIERE & VIN
SPECIAL $9.99
Coca-Cola
BIERE & VIN
SPECIAL $9.99
$9.99
ONE TIME, OUR ARMS TOUCHED AND I ALMOST FAINTED.
9.99

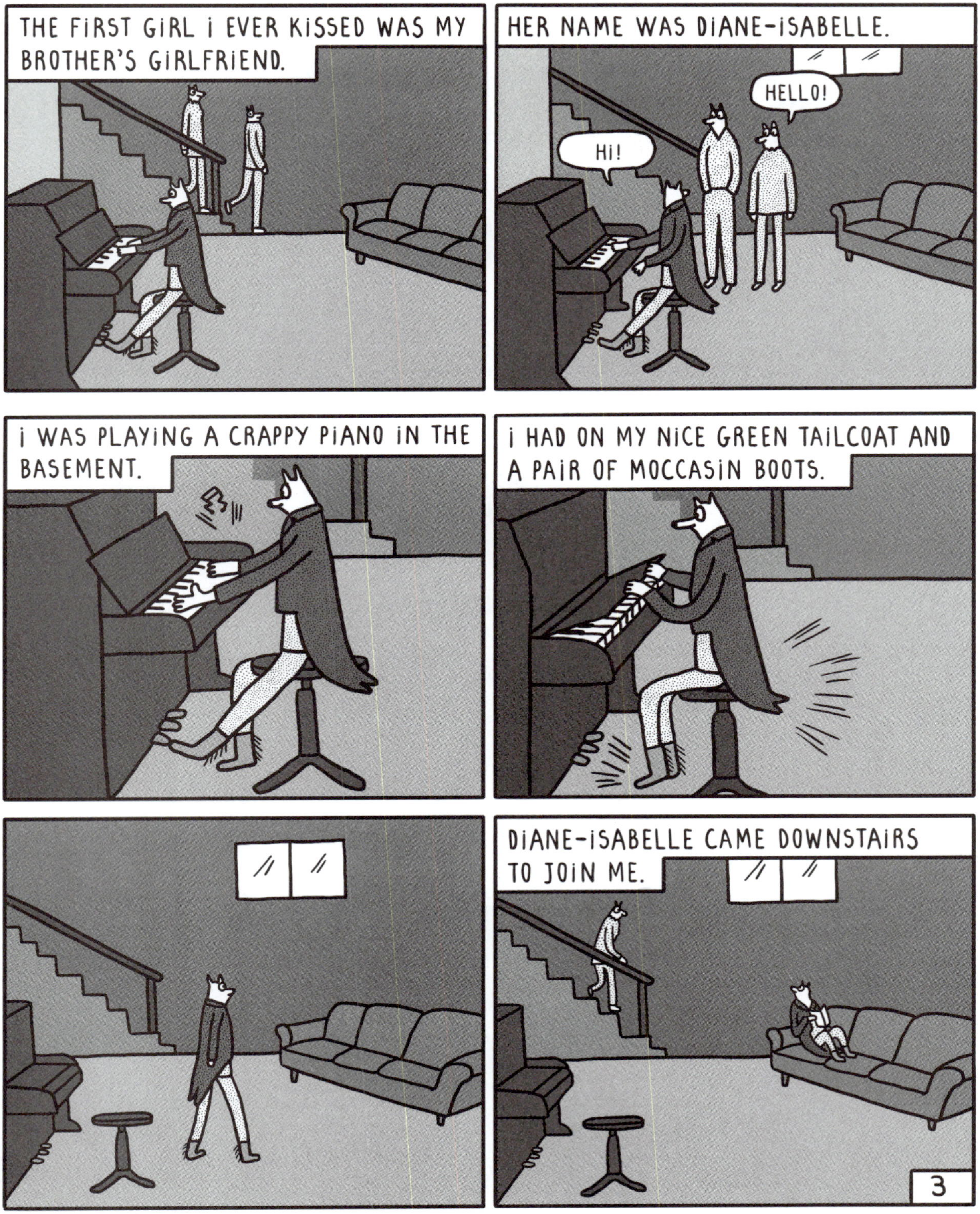
THE FIRST GIRL I EVER KISSED WAS MY BROTHER'S GIRLFRIEND.
HER NAME WAS DIANE-ISABELLE.
HELLO!
HI!
I WAS PLAYING A CRAPPY PIANO IN THE BASEMENT.
I HAD ON MY NICE GREEN TAILCOAT AND A PAIR OF MOCCASIN BOOTS.
DIANE-ISABELLE CAME DOWNSTAIRS TO JOIN ME.

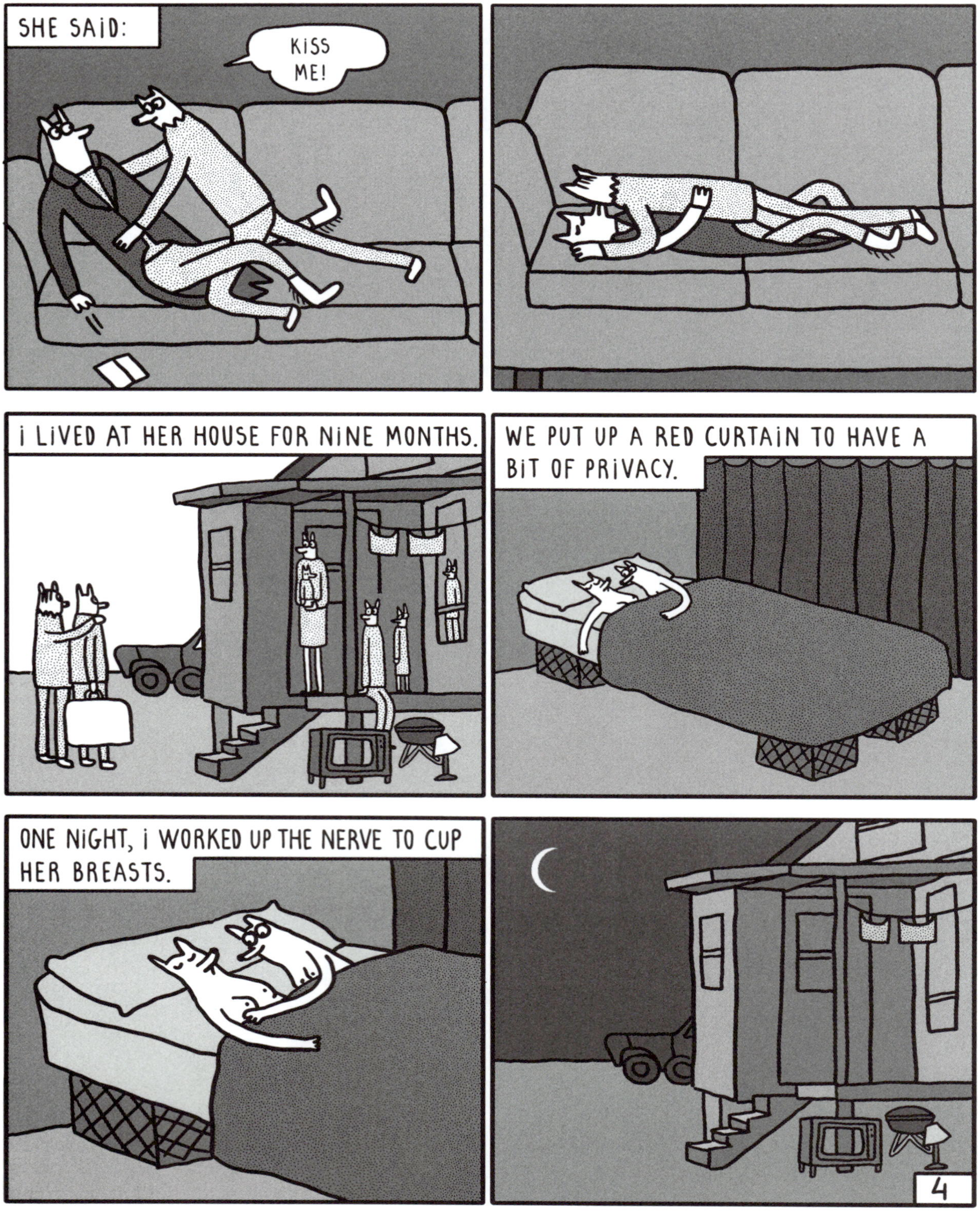
SHE SAID:
KISS ME!
I LIVED AT HER HOUSE FOR NINE MONTHS.
WE PUT UP A RED CURTAIN TO HAVE A BIT OF PRIVACY.
ONE NIGHT, I WORKED UP THE NERVE TO CUP HER BREASTS.
4

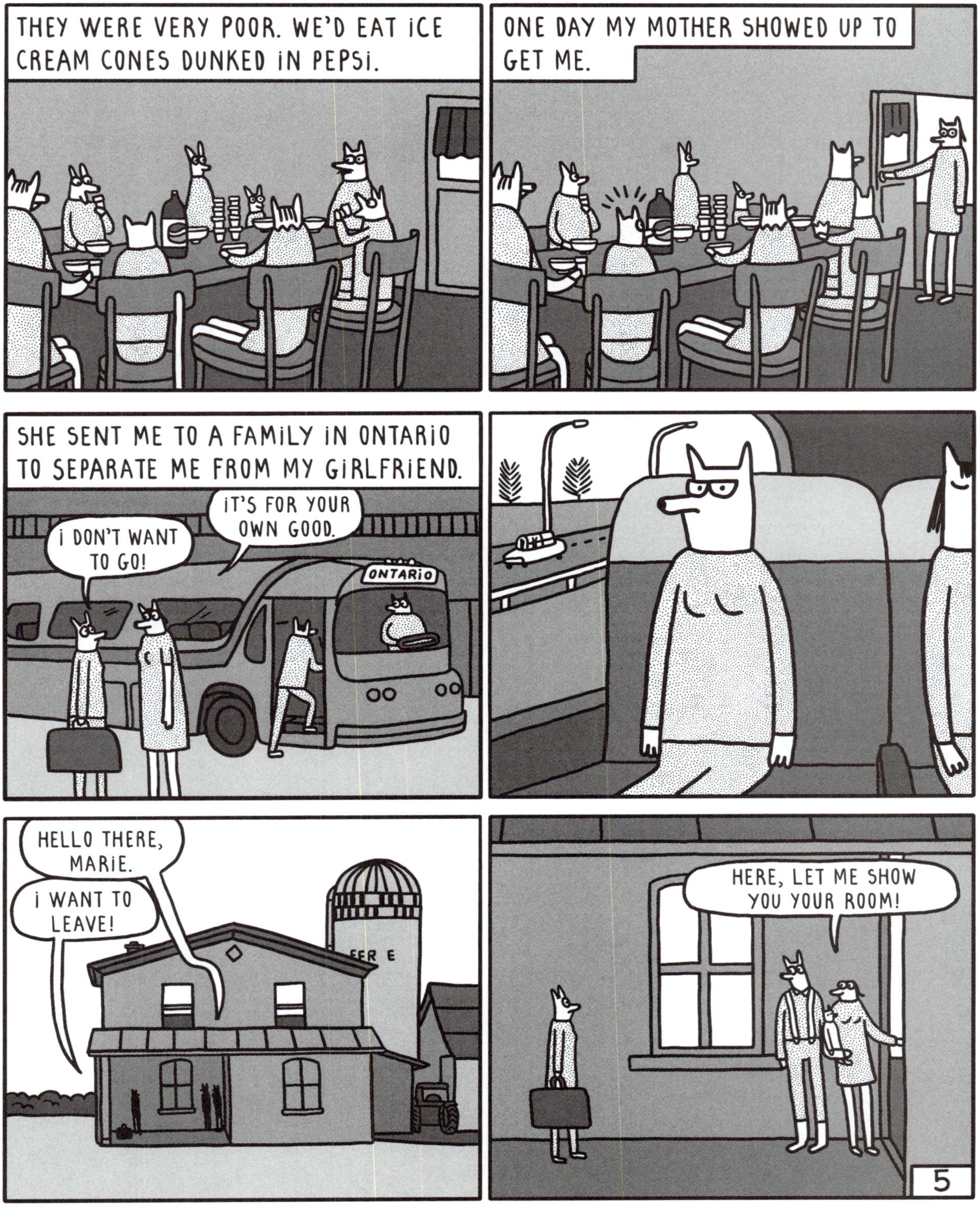
THEY WERE VERY POOR. WE'D EAT ICE CREAM CONES DUNKED IN PEPSI.
ONE DAY MY MOTHER SHOWED UP TO GET ME.
SHE SENT ME TO A FAMILY IN ONTARIO TO SEPARATE ME FROM MY GIRLFRIEND.
I DON'T WANT TO GO!
IT'S FOR YOUR OWN GOOD.
ONTARIO
HELLO THERE, MARIE.
I WANT TO LEAVE!
HERE, LET ME SHOW YOU YOUR ROOM!

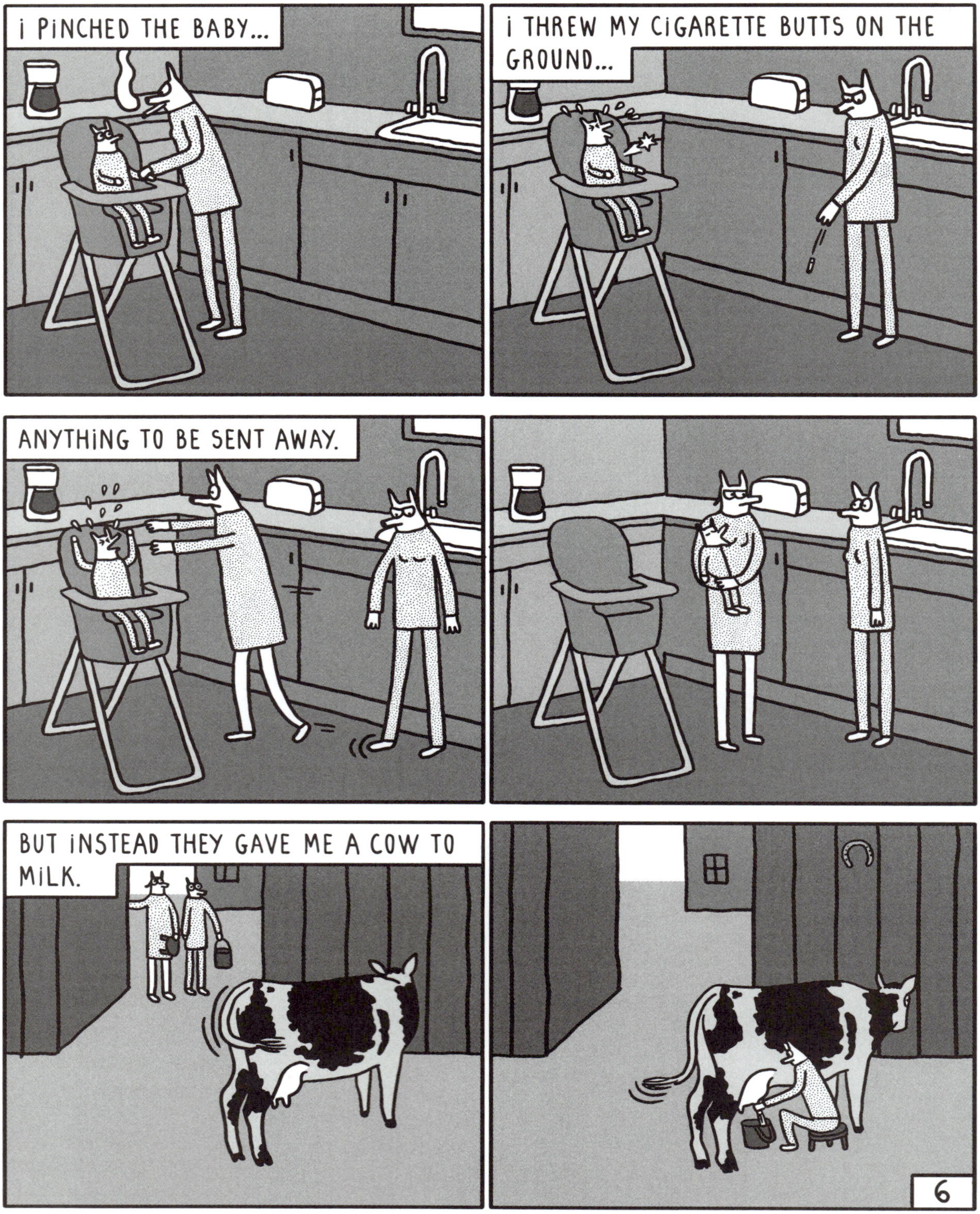
I PINCHED THE BABY...
I THREW MY CIGARETTE BUTTS ON THE GROUND...
ANYTHING TO BE SENT AWAY.
BUT INSTEAD THEY GAVE ME A COW TO MILK.

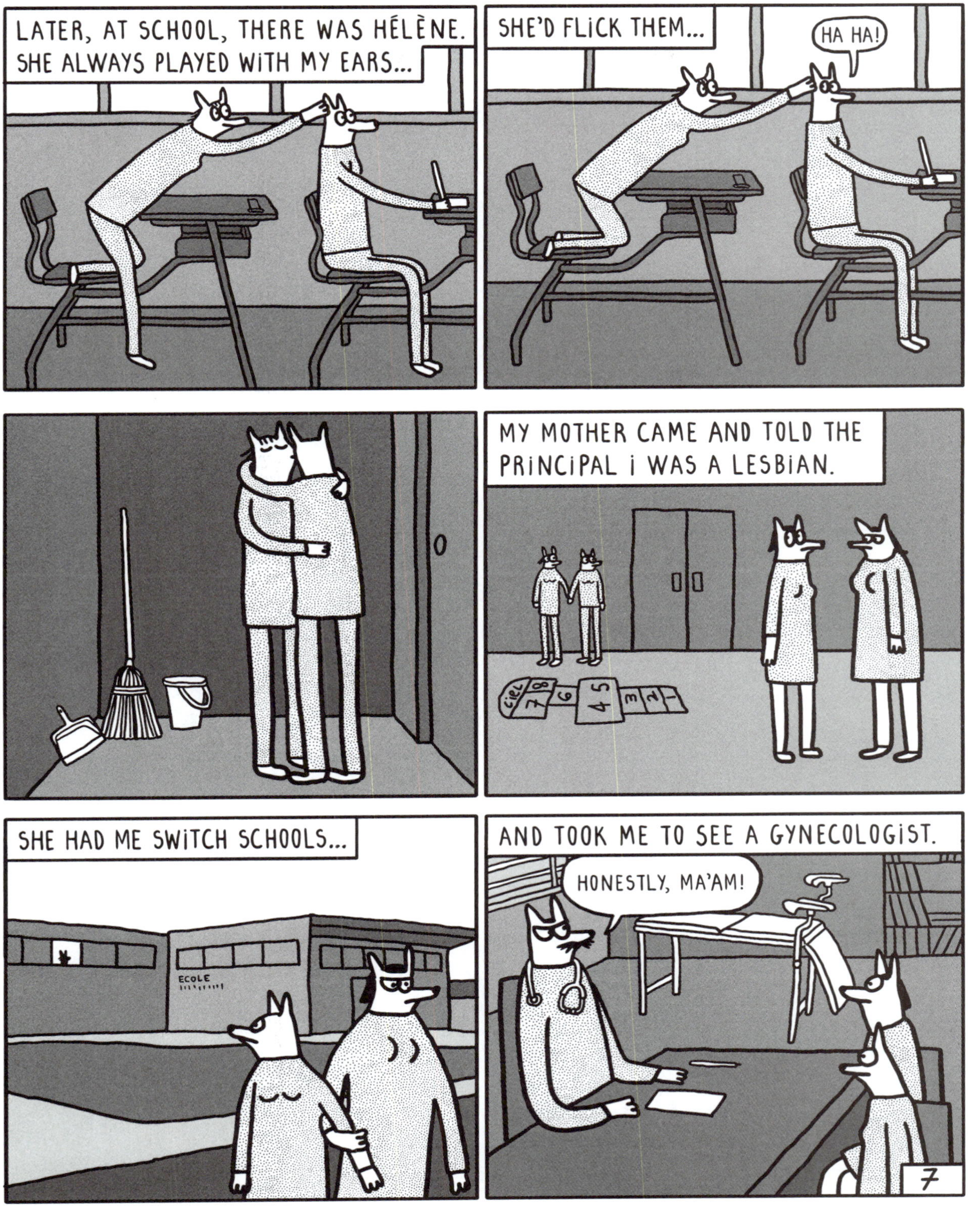
LATER, AT SCHOOL, THERE WAS HÉLÈNE. SHE ALWAYS PLAYED WITH MY EARS...
SHE'D FLICK THEM...
HA HA!
MY MOTHER CAME AND TOLD THE PRINCIPAL I WAS A LESBIAN.
SHE HAD ME SWITCH SCHOOLS...
ECOLE
AND TOOK ME TO SEE A GYNECOLOGIST.
HONESTLY, MA'AM!

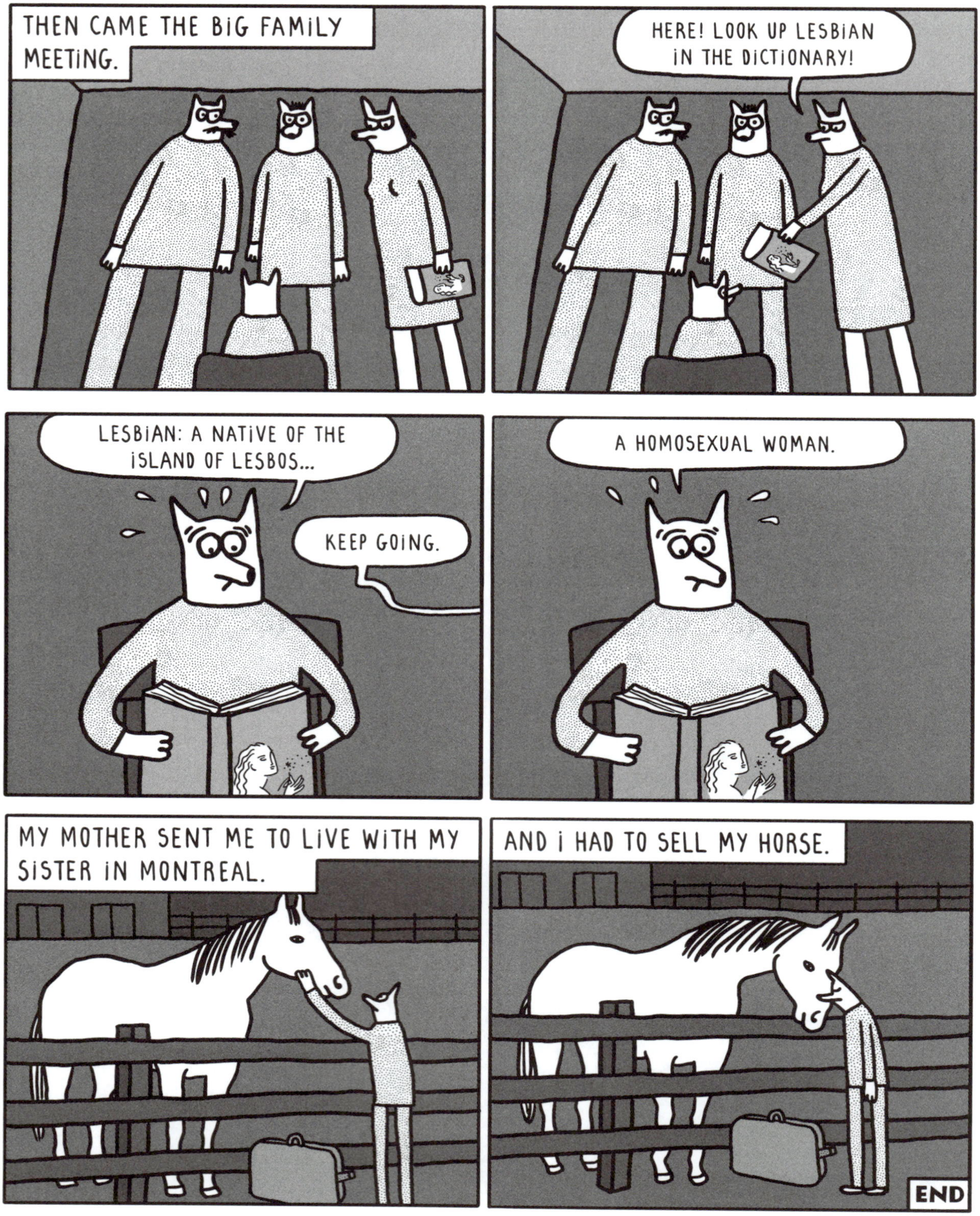
THEN CAME THE BIG FAMILY MEETING.
HERE! LOOK UP LESBIAN IN THE DICTIONARY!
LESBIAN: A NATIVE OF THE ISLAND OF LESBOS...
KEEP GOING.
A HOMOSEXUAL WOMAN.
MY MOTHER SENT ME TO LIVE WITH MY SISTER IN MONTREAL.
AND I HAD TO SELL MY HORSE.
END

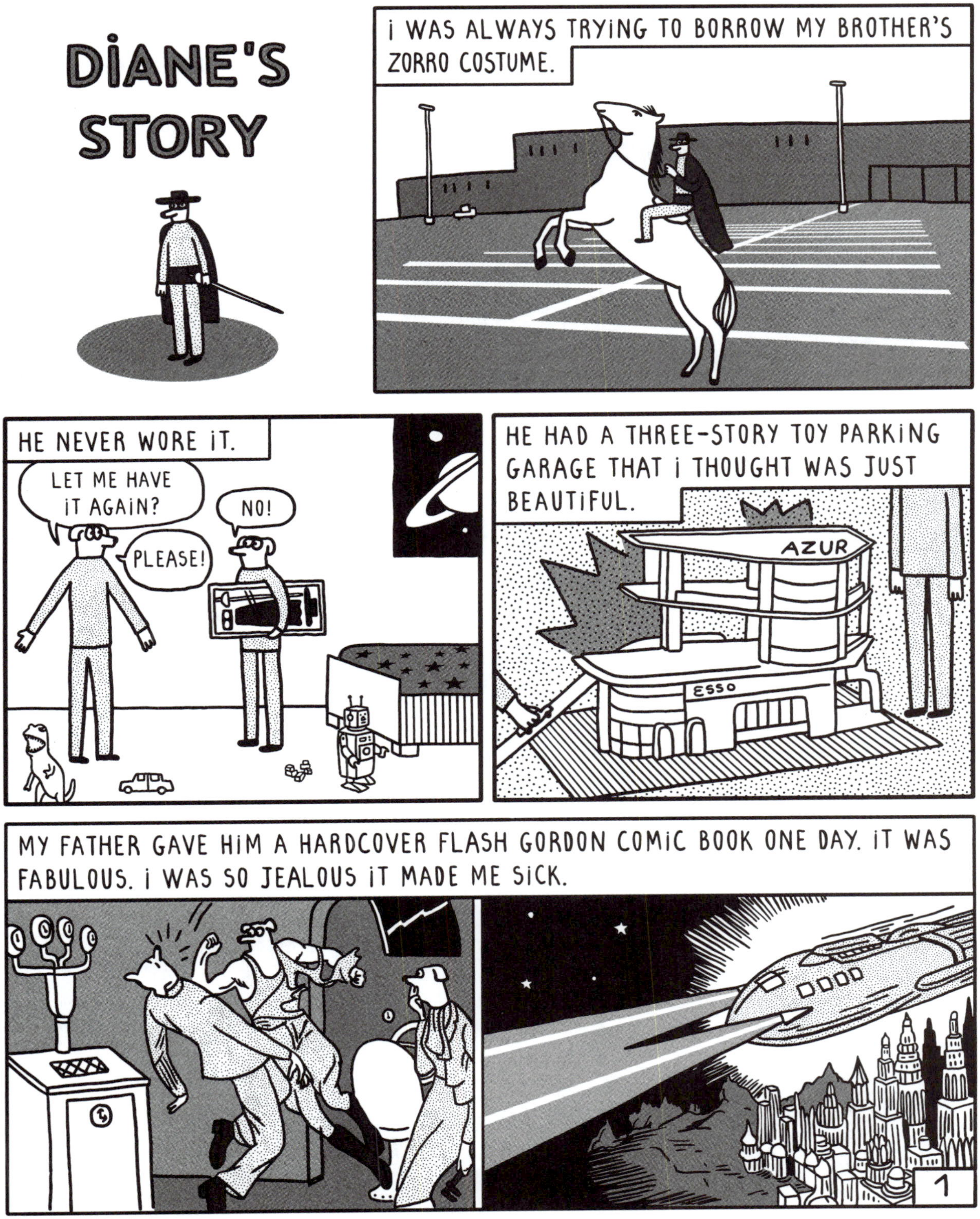
DIANE'S STORY
I WAS ALWAYS TRYING TO BORROW MY BROTHER'S ZORRO COSTUME.
HE NEVER WORE IT.
LET ME HAVE IT AGAIN?
NO!
PLEASE!
HE HAD A THREE-STORY TOY PARKING GARAGE THAT I THOUGHT WAS JUST BEAUTIFUL.
AZUR
ESSO
MY FATHER GAVE HIM A HARDCOVER FLASH GORDON COMIC BOOK ONE DAY. IT WAS FABULOUS. I WAS SO JEALOUS IT MADE ME SICK.

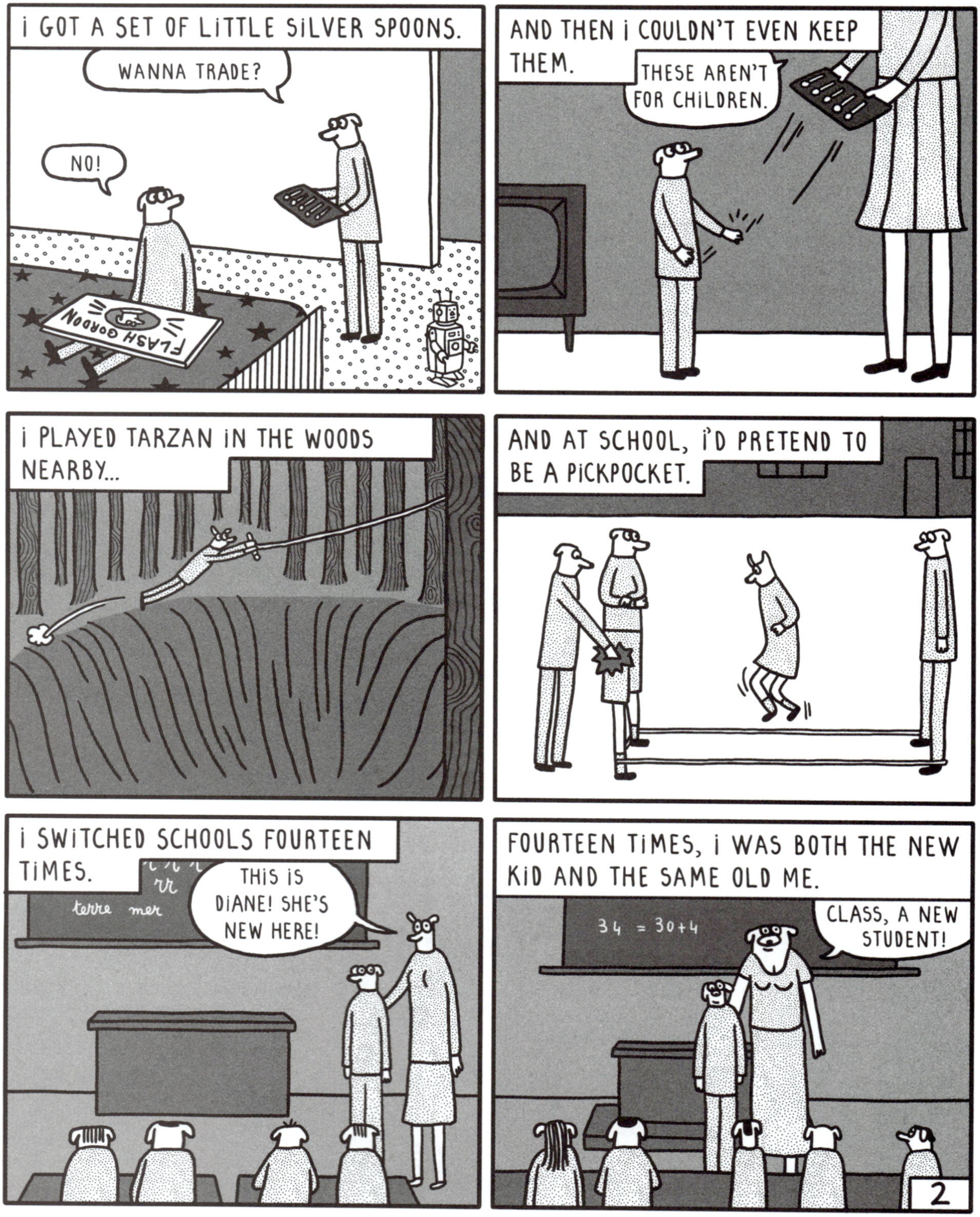
I GOT A SET OF LITTLE SILVER SPOONS.
WANNA TRADE?
NO!
FLASH GORDON
AND THEN I COULDN'T EVEN KEEP THEM.
THESE AREN'T FOR CHILDREN.
I PLAYED TARZAN IN THE WOODS NEARBY...
AND AT SCHOOL, I'D PRETEND TO BE A PICKPOCKET.
I SWITCHED SCHOOLS FOURTEEN TIMES.
terre mer
THIS IS DIANE! SHE'S NEW HERE!
FOURTEEN TIMES, I WAS BOTH THE NEW KID AND THE SAME OLD ME.
34 = 30+4
CLASS, A NEW STUDENT!

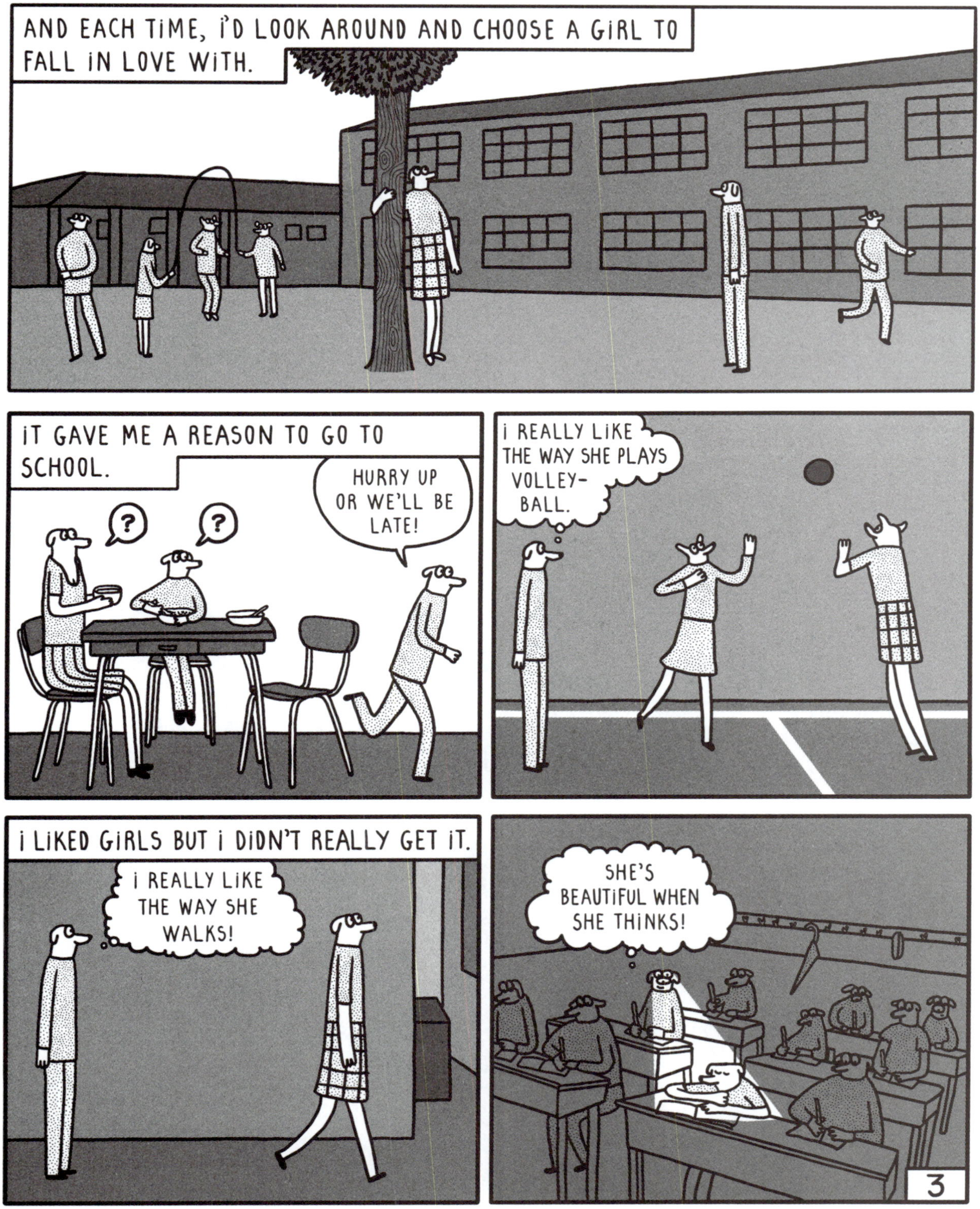
AND EACH TIME, I'D LOOK AROUND AND CHOOSE A GIRL TO FALL IN LOVE WITH.
IT GAVE ME A REASON TO GO TO SCHOOL.
?
?
HURRY UP OR WE'LL BE LATE!
I REALLY LIKE THE WAY SHE PLAYS VOLLEY-BALL.
I LIKED GIRLS BUT I DIDN'T REALLY GET IT.
I REALLY LIKE THE WAY SHE WALKS!
SHE'S BEAUTIFUL WHEN SHE THINKS!

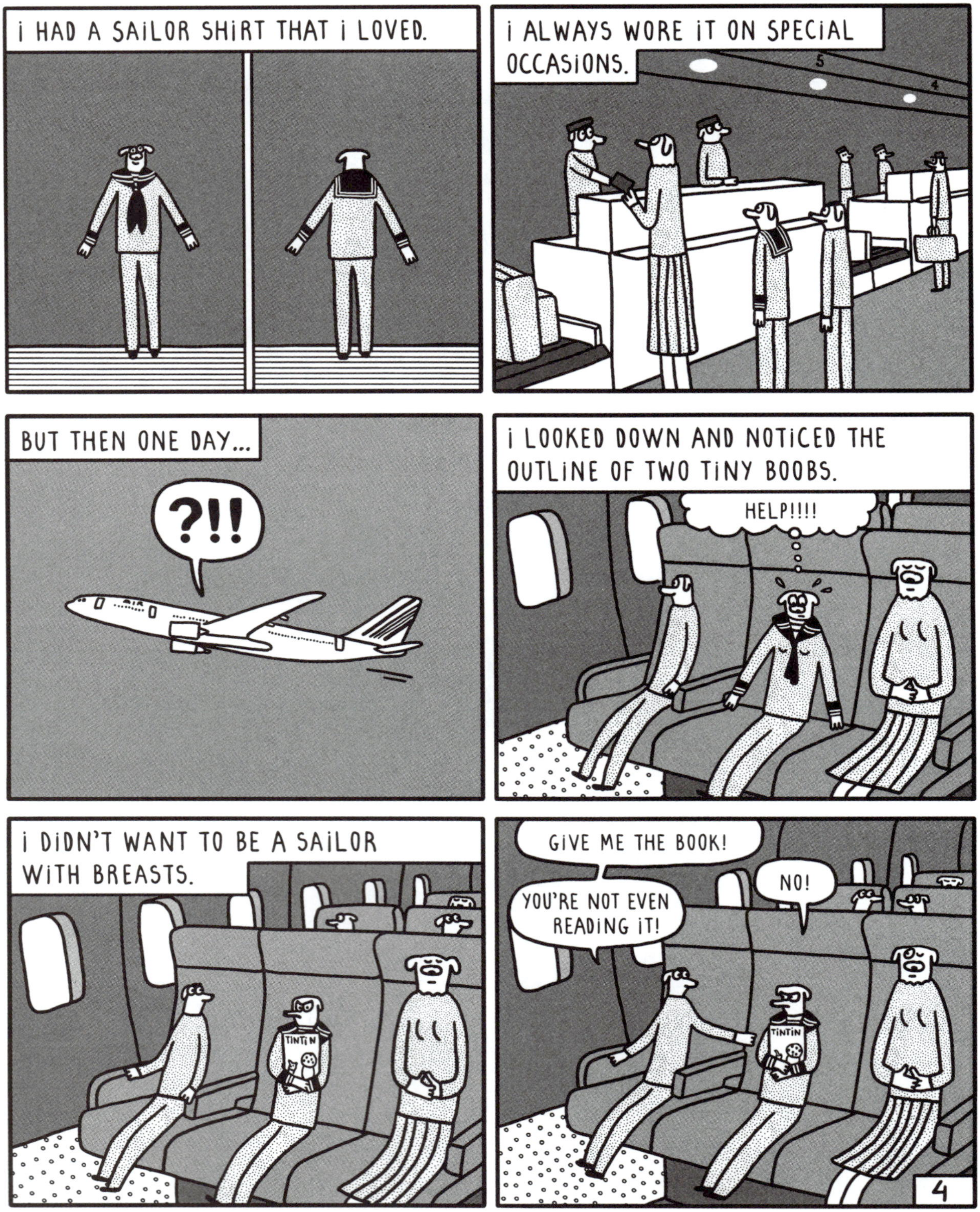
i HAD A SAiLOR SHiRT THAT i LOVED.
i ALWAYS WORE iT ON SPECiAL OCCASiONS.
5
4
BUT THEN ONE DAY...
?!!
i LOOKED DOWN AND NOTiCED THE OUTLiNE OF TWO TiNY BOOBS.
HELP!!!!
i DiDN'T WANT TO BE A SAiLOR WiTH BREASTS.
TiNTiN
GiVE ME THE BOOK!
YOU'RE NOT EVEN READiNG iT!
NO!
TiNTiN

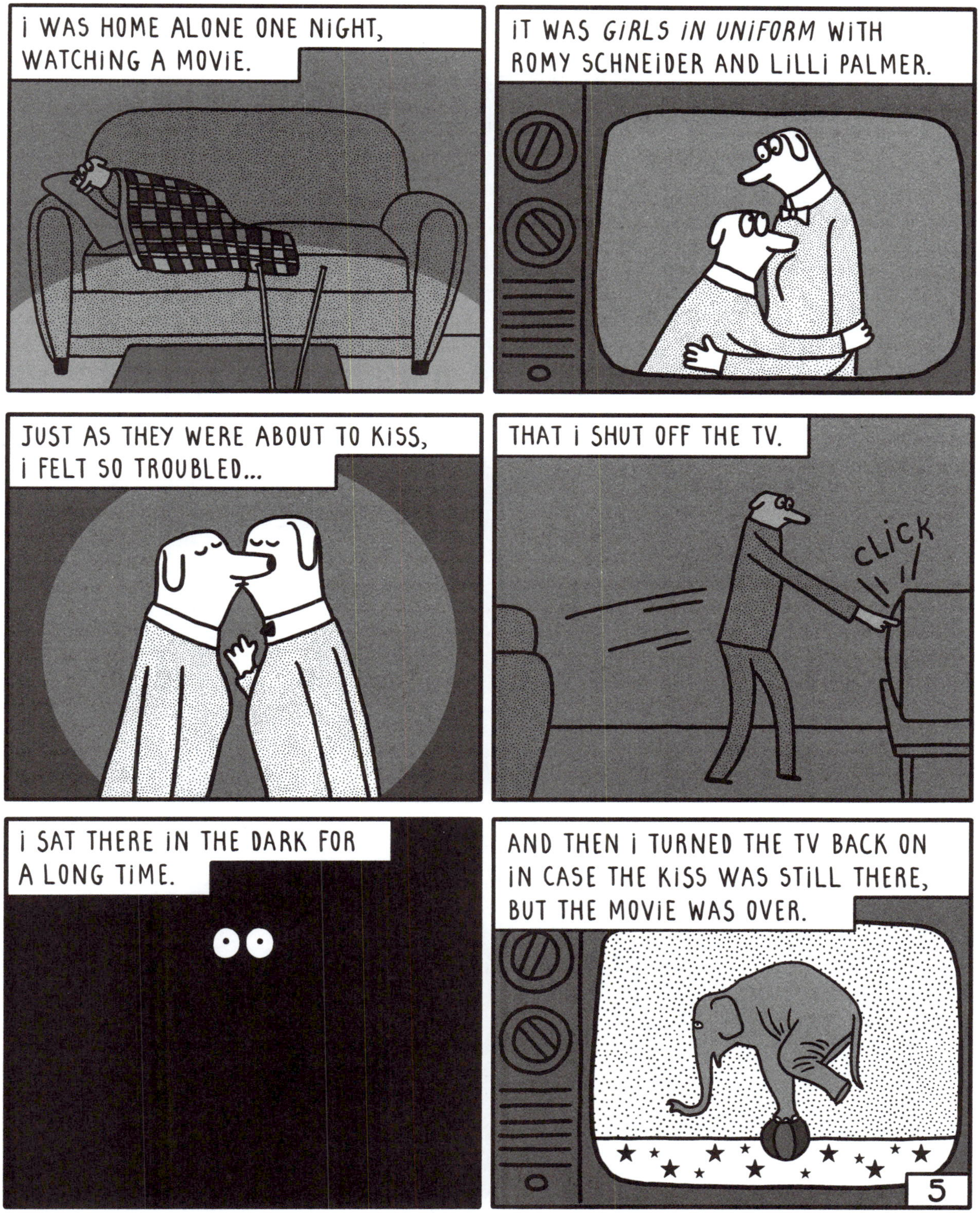
I WAS HOME ALONE ONE NIGHT, WATCHING A MOVIE.
IT WAS *GIRLS IN UNIFORM* WITH ROMY SCHNEIDER AND LILLI PALMER.
JUST AS THEY WERE ABOUT TO KISS, I FELT SO TROUBLED...
THAT I SHUT OFF THE TV.
CLICK
I SAT THERE IN THE DARK FOR A LONG TIME.
AND THEN I TURNED THE TV BACK ON IN CASE THE KISS WAS STILL THERE, BUT THE MOVIE WAS OVER.

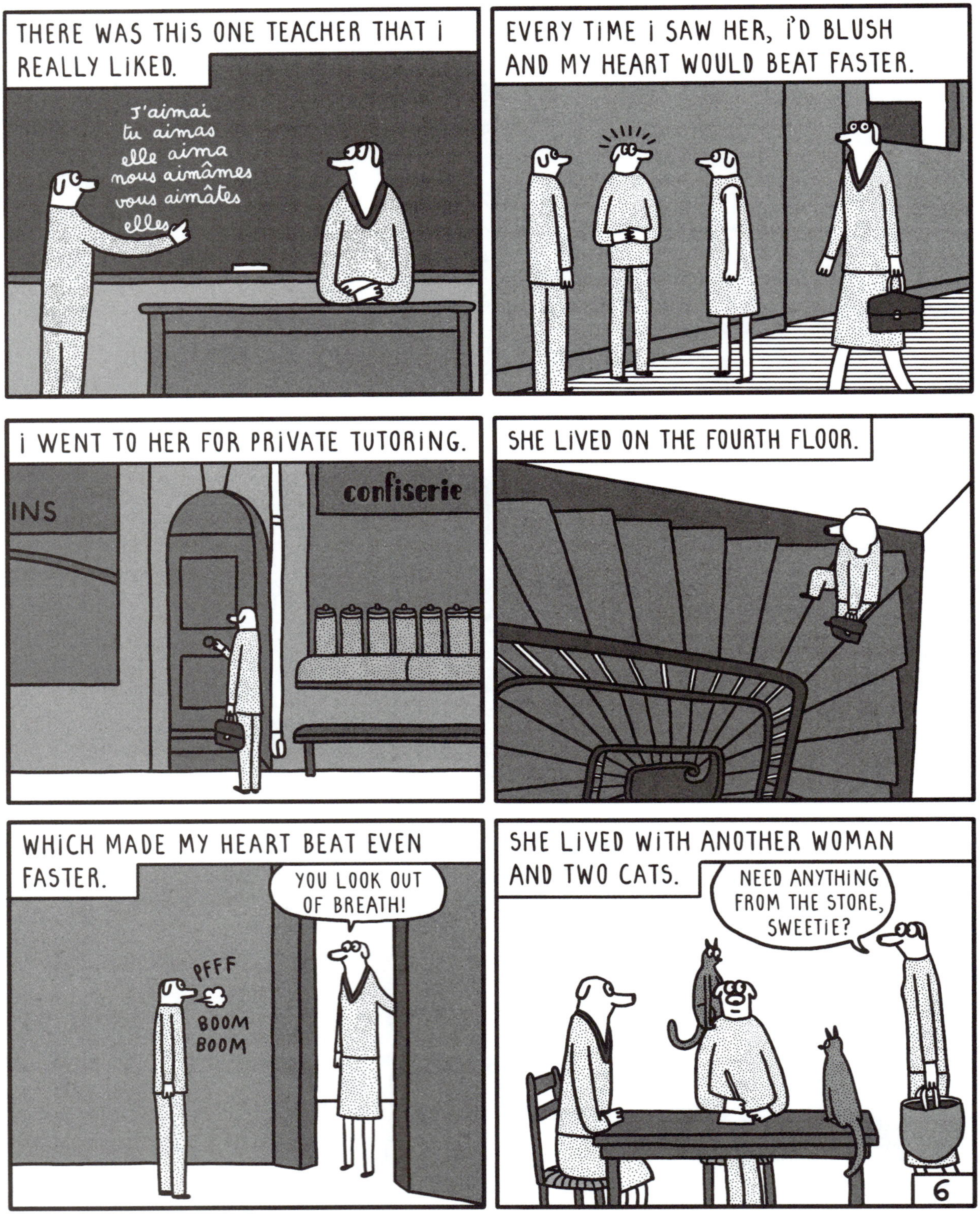
THERE WAS THIS ONE TEACHER THAT i REALLY LiKED.
J'aimai
tu aimas
elle aima
nous aimâmes
vous aimâtes
elles
EVERY TiME i SAW HER, i'D BLUSH AND MY HEART WOULD BEAT FASTER.
i WENT TO HER FOR PRiVATE TUTORiNG.
INS
confiserie
SHE LiVED ON THE FOURTH FLOOR.
WHiCH MADE MY HEART BEAT EVEN FASTER.
YOU LOOK OUT OF BREATH!
PFFF
BOOM BOOM
SHE LiVED WiTH ANOTHER WOMAN AND TWO CATS.
NEED ANYTHiNG FROM THE STORE, SWEETiE?

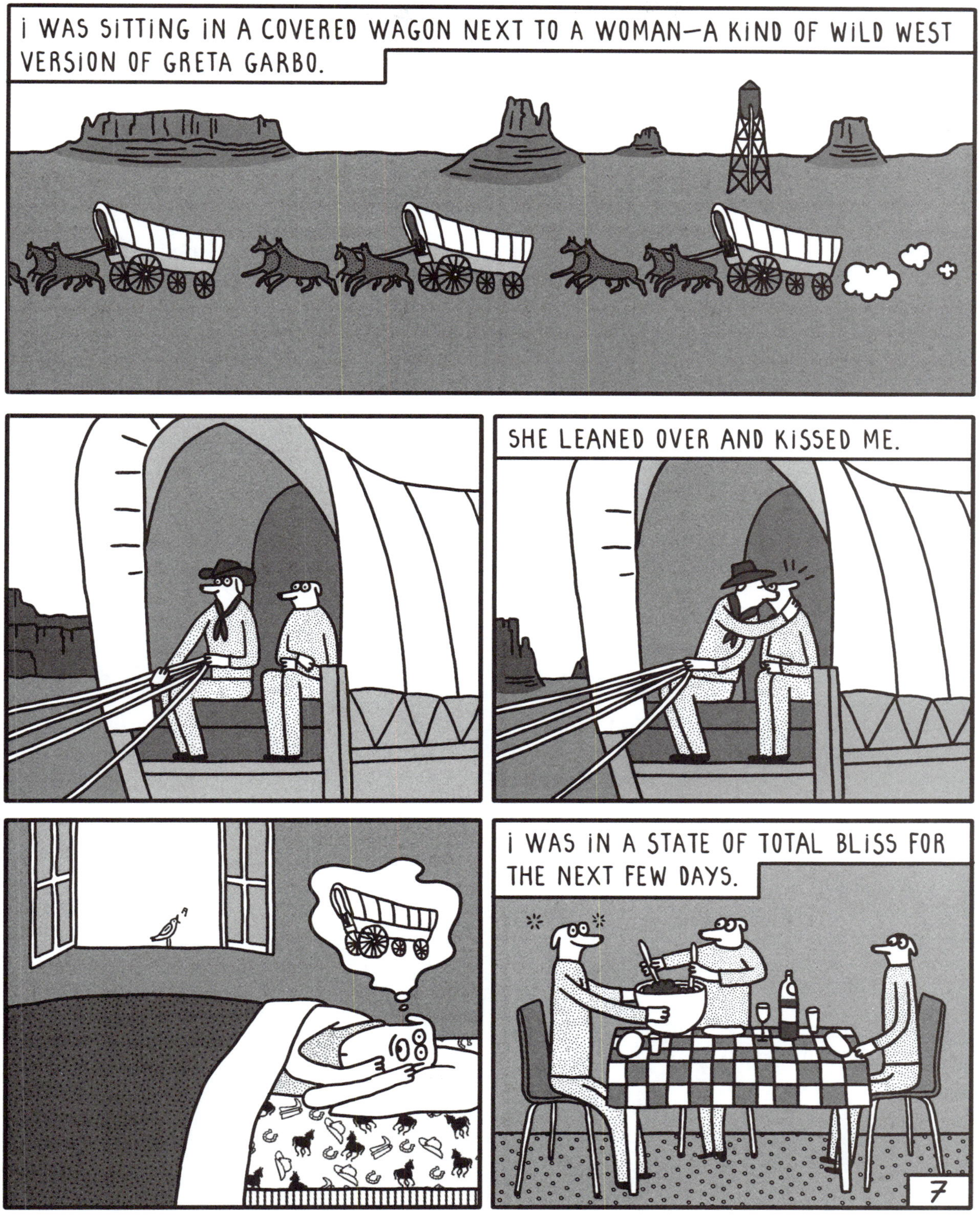
I WAS SITTING IN A COVERED WAGON NEXT TO A WOMAN—A KIND OF WILD WEST VERSION OF GRETA GARBO.
SHE LEANED OVER AND KISSED ME.
I WAS IN A STATE OF TOTAL BLISS FOR THE NEXT FEW DAYS.
7

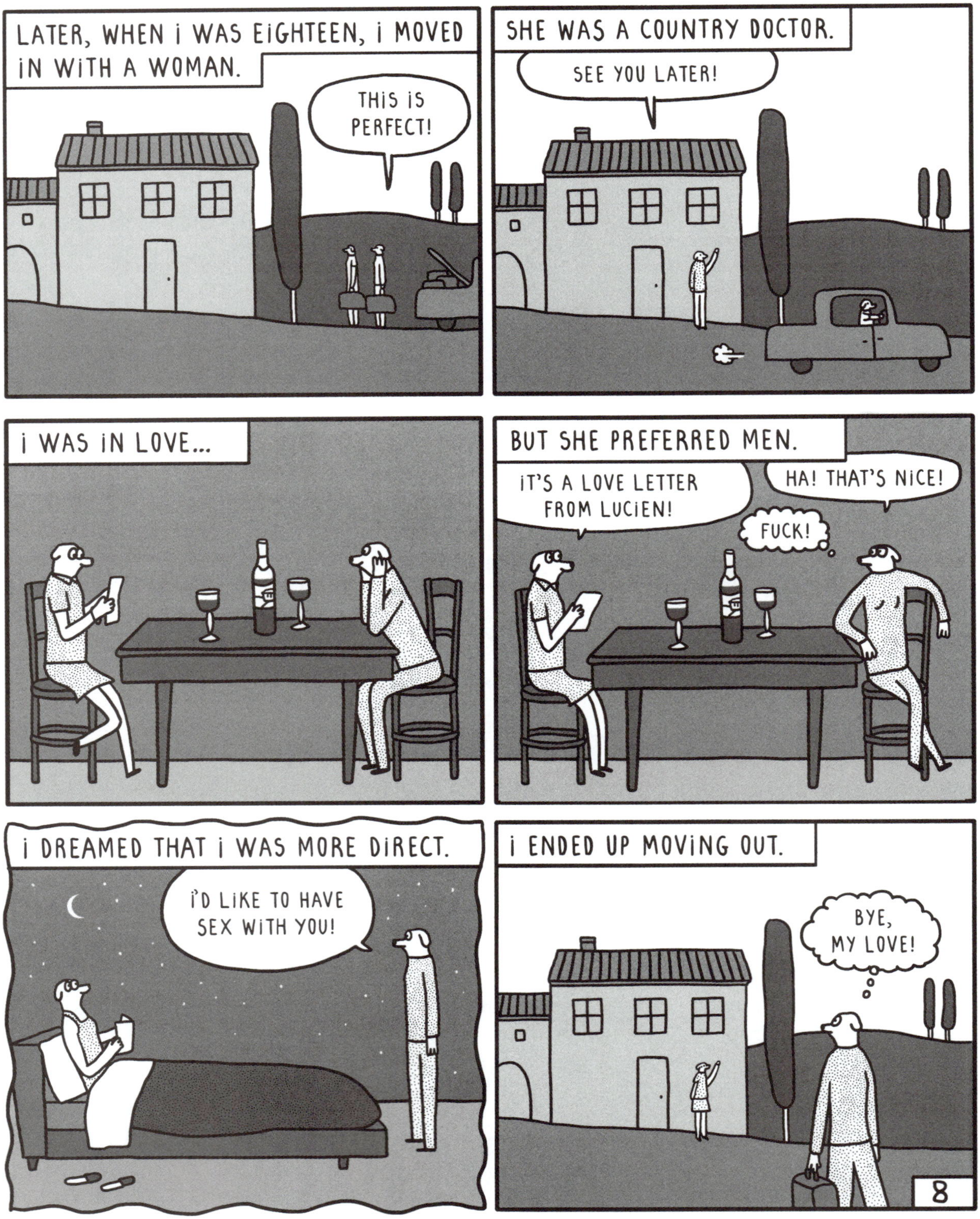
LATER, WHEN I WAS EIGHTEEN, I MOVED IN WITH A WOMAN.
THIS IS PERFECT!
SHE WAS A COUNTRY DOCTOR.
SEE YOU LATER!
I WAS IN LOVE...
BUT SHE PREFERRED MEN.
IT'S A LOVE LETTER FROM LUCIEN!
HA! THAT'S NICE!
FUCK!
I DREAMED THAT I WAS MORE DIRECT.
I'D LIKE TO HAVE SEX WITH YOU!
I ENDED UP MOVING OUT.
BYE, MY LOVE!
8

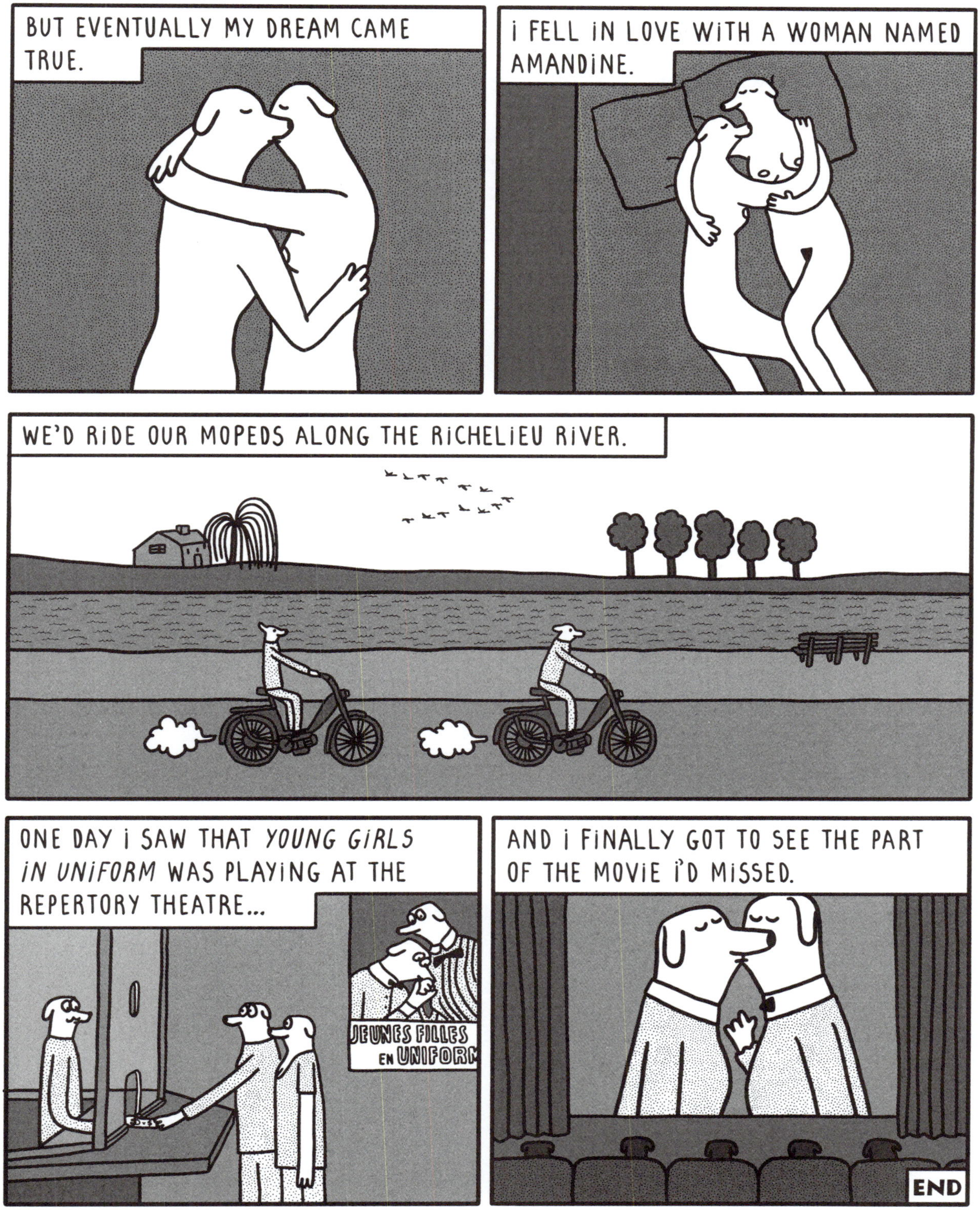
BUT EVENTUALLY MY DREAM CAME TRUE.
I FELL IN LOVE WITH A WOMAN NAMED AMANDINE.
WE'D RIDE OUR MOPEDS ALONG THE RICHELIEU RIVER.
ONE DAY I SAW THAT *YOUNG GIRLS IN UNIFORM* WAS PLAYING AT THE REPERTORY THEATRE...
JEUNES FILLES EN UNIFORM
AND I FINALLY GOT TO SEE THE PART OF THE MOVIE I'D MISSED.
END

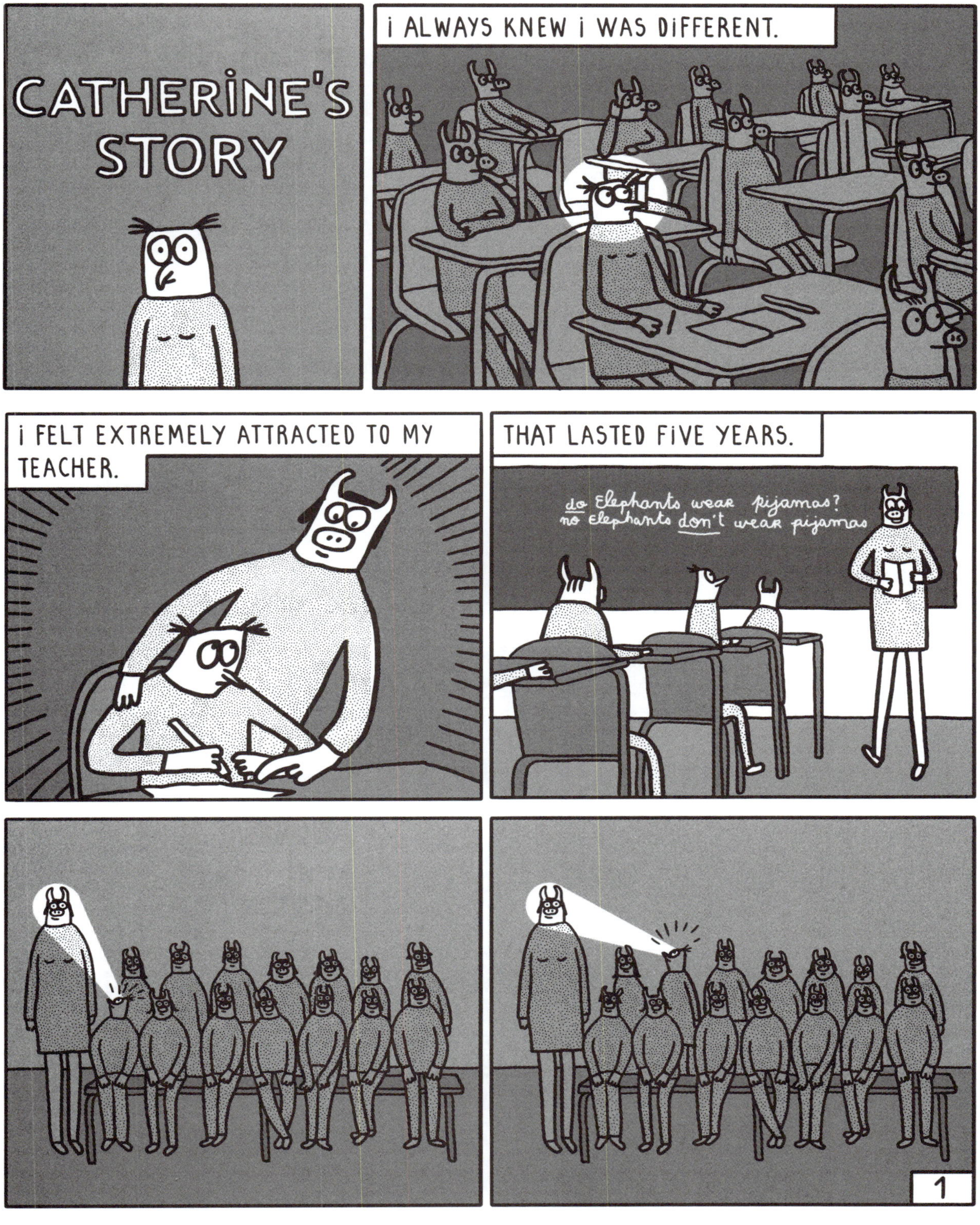
CATHERINE'S STORY
I ALWAYS KNEW I WAS DIFFERENT.
I FELT EXTREMELY ATTRACTED TO MY TEACHER.
THAT LASTED FIVE YEARS.
do Elephants wear pijamas?
no Elephants don't wear pijamas

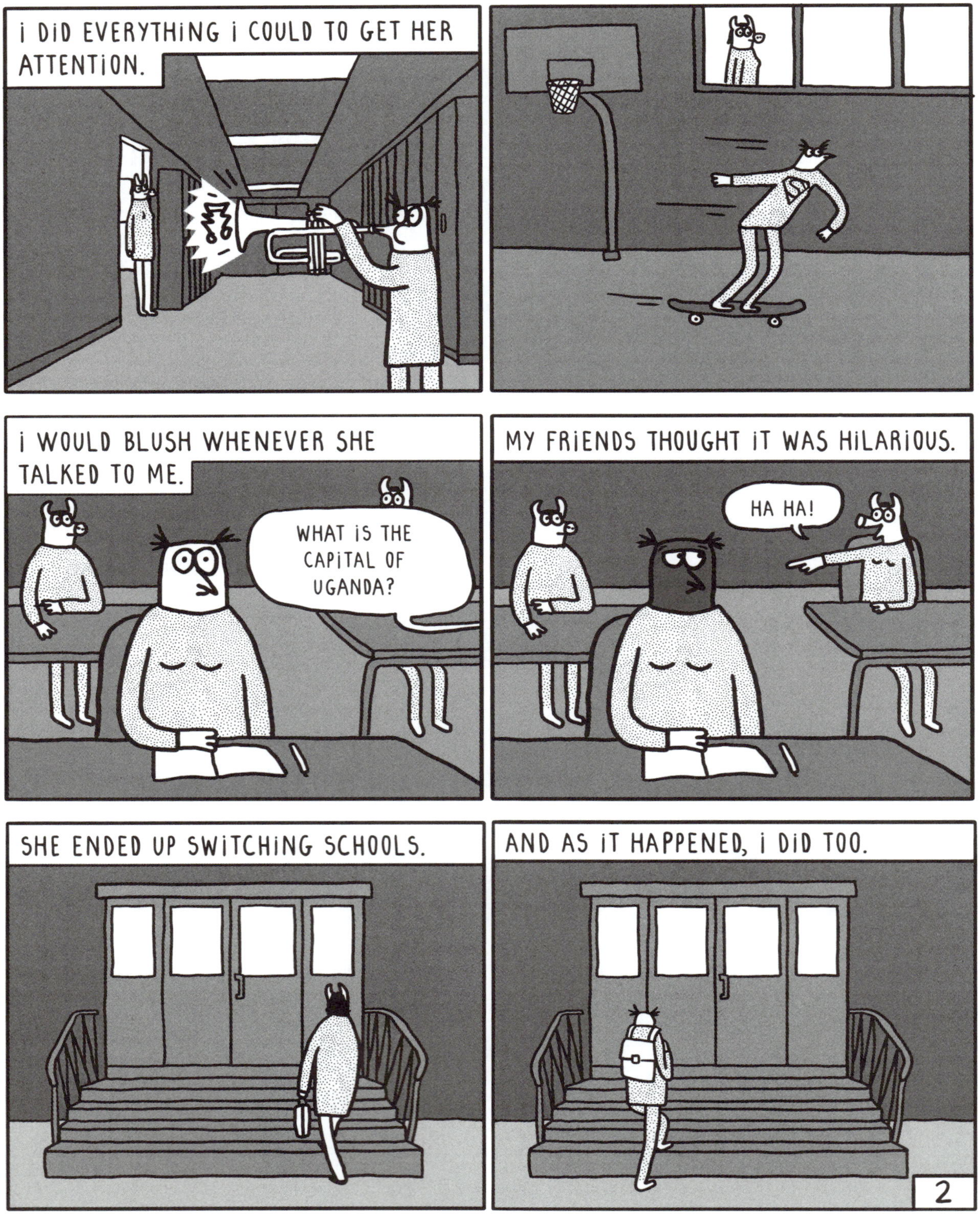
I DID EVERYTHING I COULD TO GET HER ATTENTION.
I WOULD BLUSH WHENEVER SHE TALKED TO ME.
WHAT IS THE CAPITAL OF UGANDA?
MY FRIENDS THOUGHT IT WAS HILARIOUS.
HA HA!
SHE ENDED UP SWITCHING SCHOOLS.
AND AS IT HAPPENED, I DID TOO.

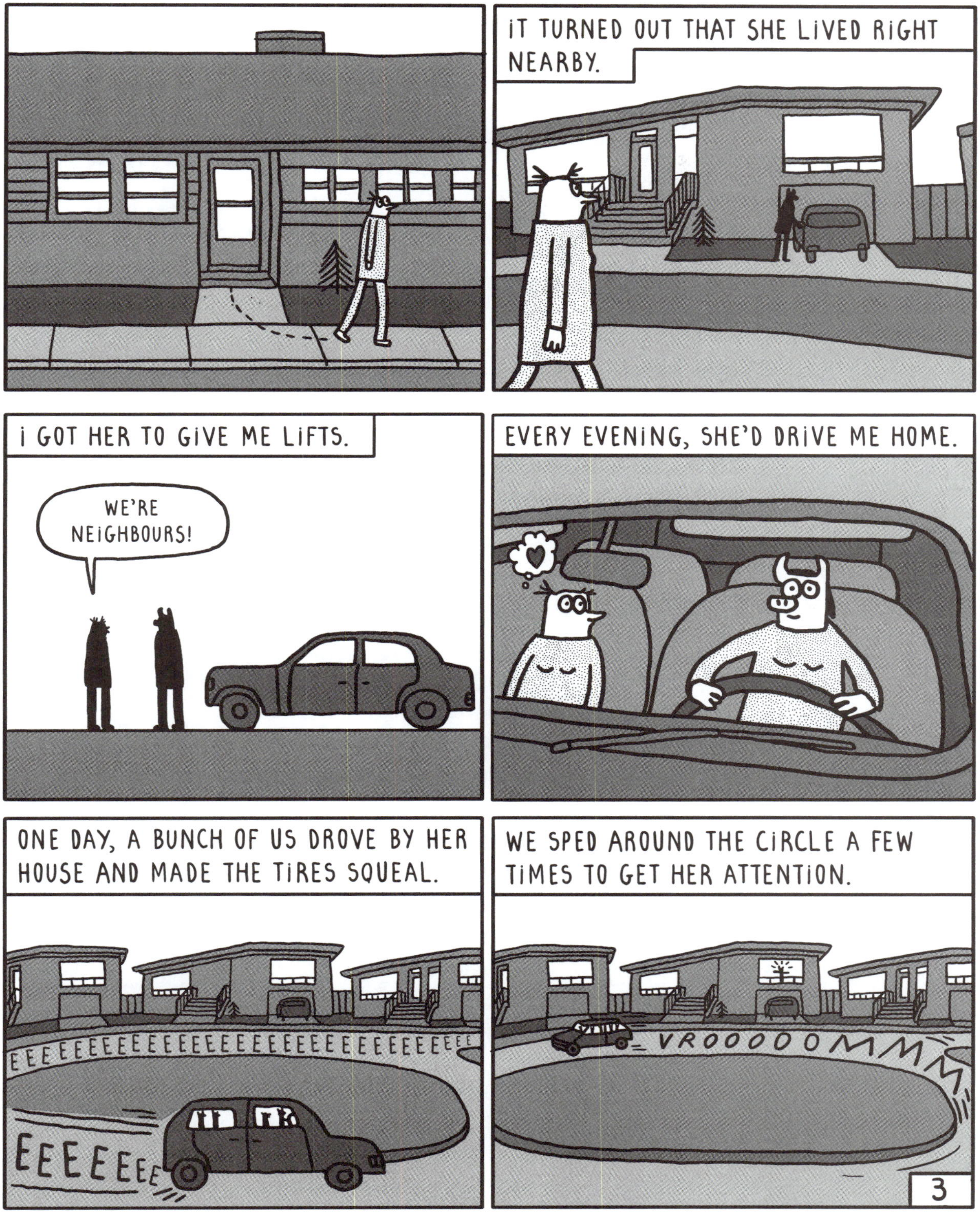

IT TURNED OUT THAT SHE LIVED RIGHT NEARBY.
I GOT HER TO GIVE ME LIFTS.
WE'RE NEIGHBOURS!
EVERY EVENING, SHE'D DRIVE ME HOME.
ONE DAY, A BUNCH OF US DROVE BY HER HOUSE AND MADE THE TIRES SQUEAL.
EEEEEEEEEEEEEEEEEEEEEEEEEEEEEEEEEEEE
EEEEEEEE
WE SPED AROUND THE CIRCLE A FEW TIMES TO GET HER ATTENTION.
VROOOOOOMMMM

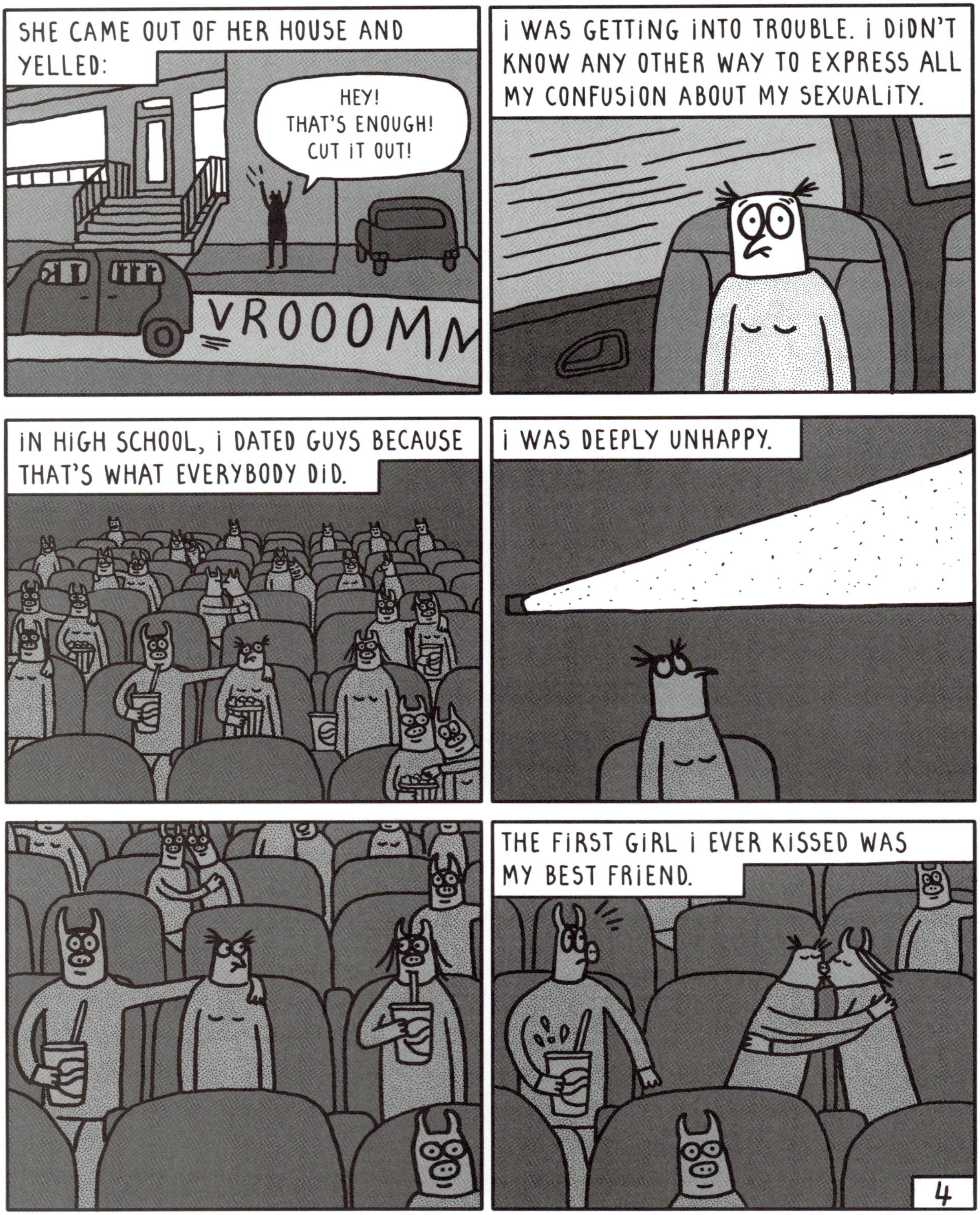
SHE CAME OUT OF HER HOUSE AND YELLED:
HEY! THAT'S ENOUGH! CUT iT OUT!
VROOOMM
i WAS GETTiNG iNTO TROUBLE. i DiDN'T KNOW ANY OTHER WAY TO EXPRESS ALL MY CONFUSiON ABOUT MY SEXUALiTY.
iN HiGH SCHOOL, i DATED GUYS BECAUSE THAT'S WHAT EVERYBODY DiD.
i WAS DEEPLY UNHAPPY.
THE FiRST GiRL i EVER KiSSED WAS MY BEST FRiEND.

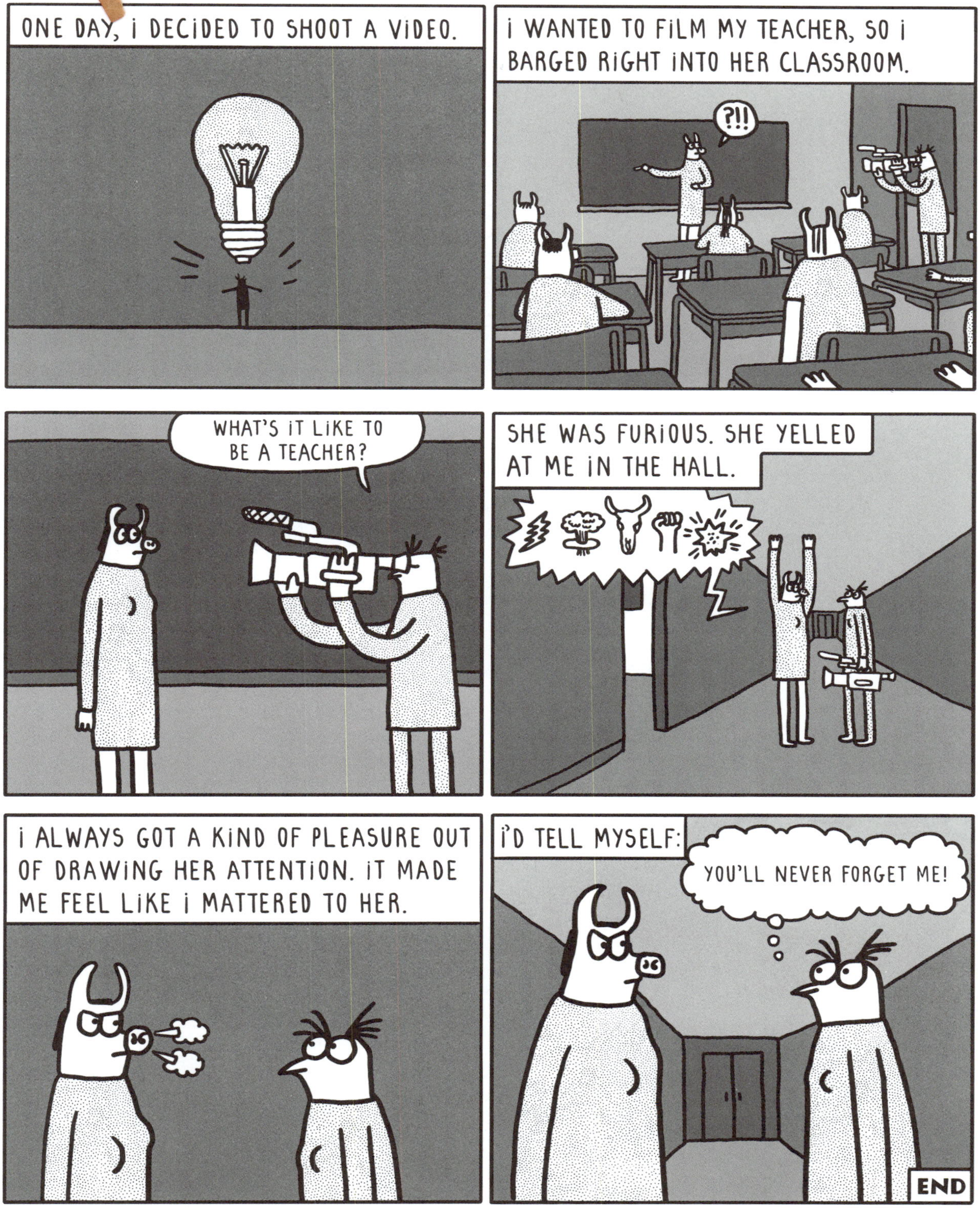
ONE DAY, I DECIDED TO SHOOT A VIDEO.
I WANTED TO FILM MY TEACHER, SO I BARGED RIGHT INTO HER CLASSROOM.
?!!
WHAT'S IT LIKE TO BE A TEACHER?
SHE WAS FURIOUS. SHE YELLED AT ME IN THE HALL.
I ALWAYS GOT A KIND OF PLEASURE OUT OF DRAWING HER ATTENTION. IT MADE ME FEEL LIKE I MATTERED TO HER.
I'D TELL MYSELF:
YOU'LL NEVER FORGET ME!
END

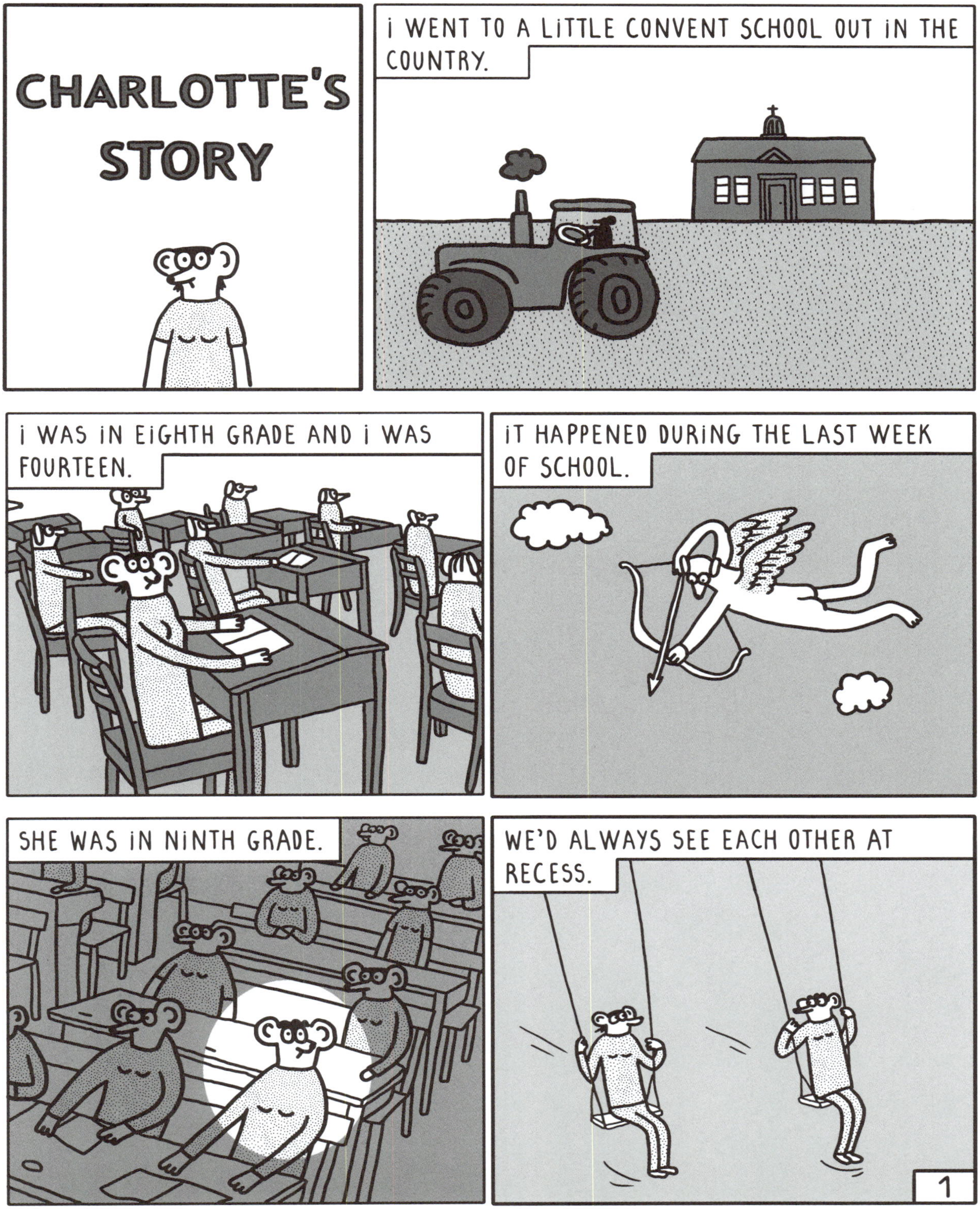
CHARLOTTE'S STORY
I WENT TO A LITTLE CONVENT SCHOOL OUT IN THE COUNTRY.
I WAS IN EIGHTH GRADE AND I WAS FOURTEEN.
IT HAPPENED DURING THE LAST WEEK OF SCHOOL.
SHE WAS IN NINTH GRADE.
WE'D ALWAYS SEE EACH OTHER AT RECESS.
1

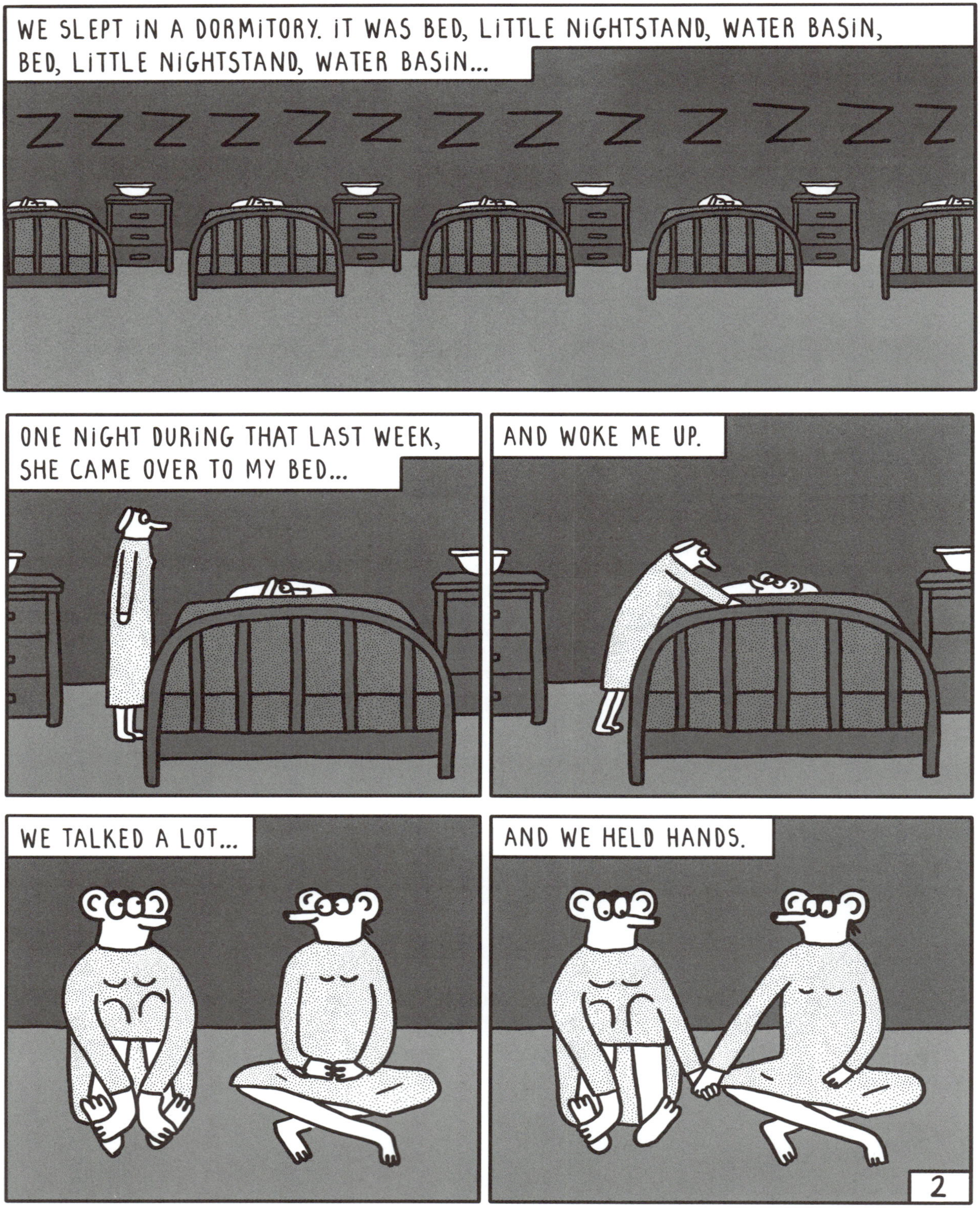
WE SLEPT IN A DORMITORY. IT WAS BED, LITTLE NIGHTSTAND, WATER BASIN, BED, LITTLE NIGHTSTAND, WATER BASIN...
ZZZZZZZZZZZZZZ
ONE NIGHT DURING THAT LAST WEEK, SHE CAME OVER TO MY BED...
AND WOKE ME UP.
WE TALKED A LOT...
AND WE HELD HANDS.

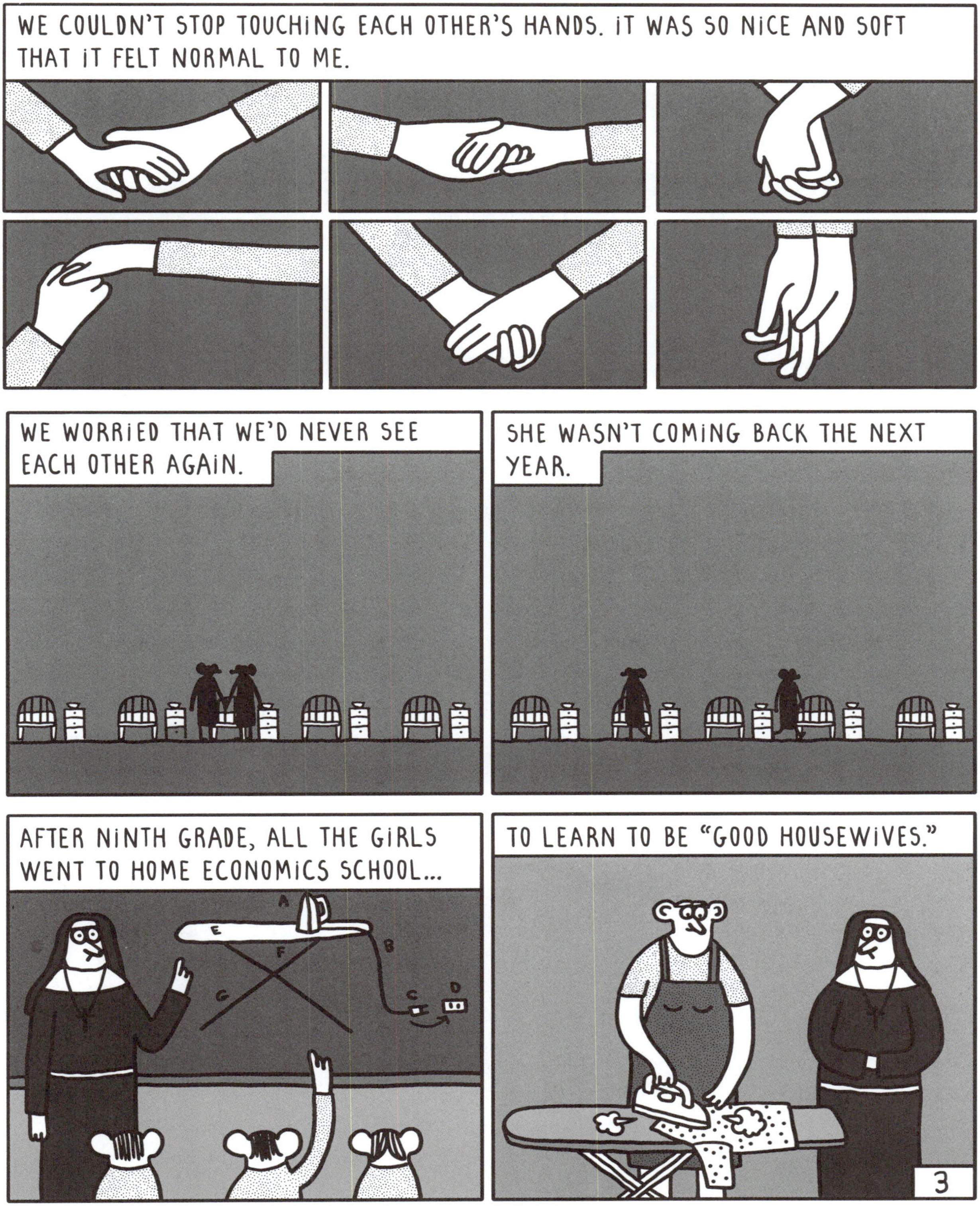
WE COULDN'T STOP TOUCHING EACH OTHER'S HANDS. IT WAS SO NICE AND SOFT THAT IT FELT NORMAL TO ME.
WE WORRIED THAT WE'D NEVER SEE EACH OTHER AGAIN.
SHE WASN'T COMING BACK THE NEXT YEAR.
AFTER NINTH GRADE, ALL THE GIRLS WENT TO HOME ECONOMICS SCHOOL...
A
E
F
B
G
C
D
TO LEARN TO BE "GOOD HOUSEWIVES."

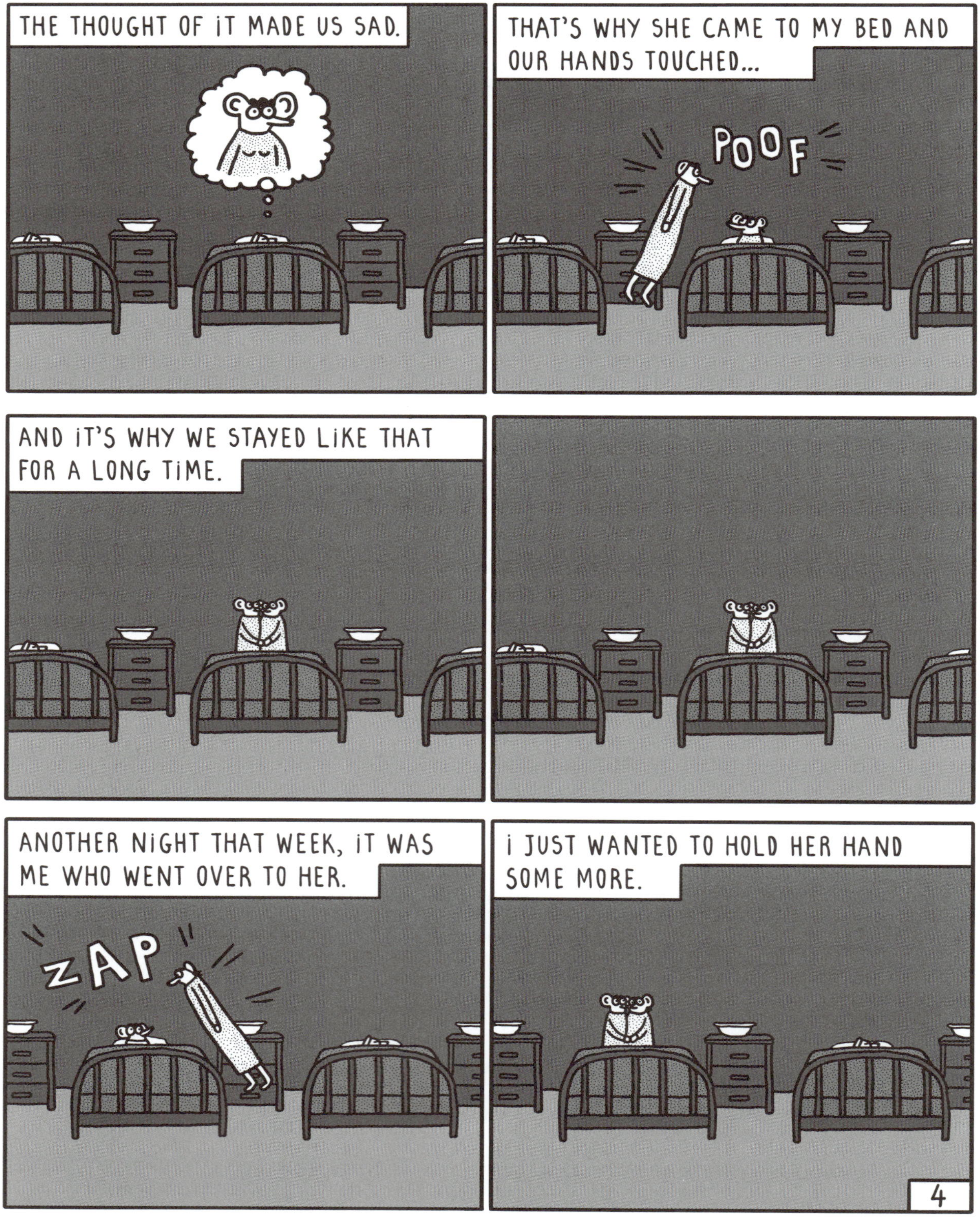
THE THOUGHT OF iT MADE US SAD.
THAT'S WHY SHE CAME TO MY BED AND OUR HANDS TOUCHED...
POOF
AND iT'S WHY WE STAYED LiKE THAT FOR A LONG TiME.
ANOTHER NiGHT THAT WEEK, iT WAS ME WHO WENT OVER TO HER.
ZAP
i JUST WANTED TO HOLD HER HAND SOME MORE.

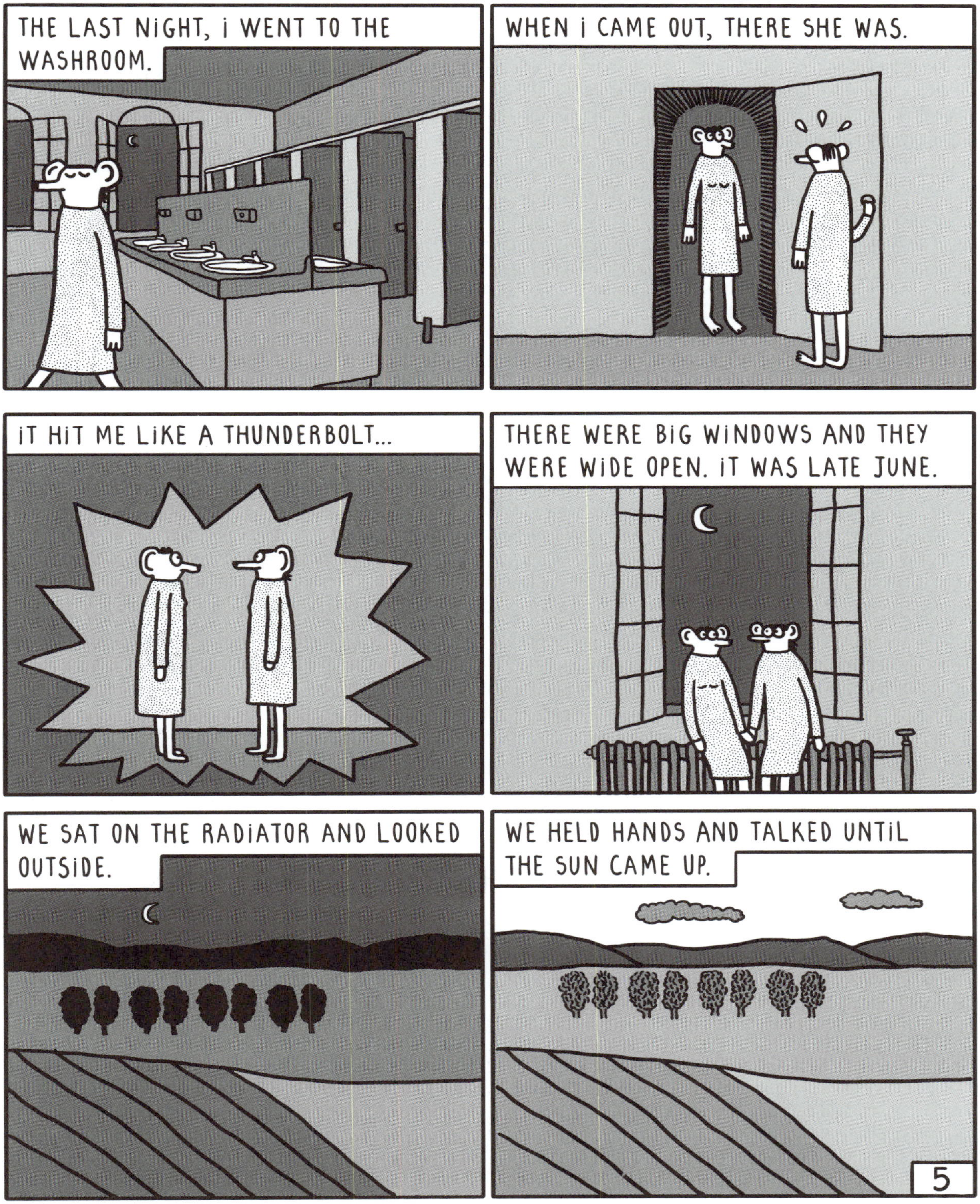
THE LAST NiGHT, i WENT TO THE WASHROOM.
WHEN i CAME OUT, THERE SHE WAS.
iT HiT ME LiKE A THUNDERBOLT...
THERE WERE BiG WiNDOWS AND THEY WERE WiDE OPEN. iT WAS LATE JUNE.
WE SAT ON THE RADiATOR AND LOOKED OUTSiDE.
WE HELD HANDS AND TALKED UNTiL THE SUN CAME UP.

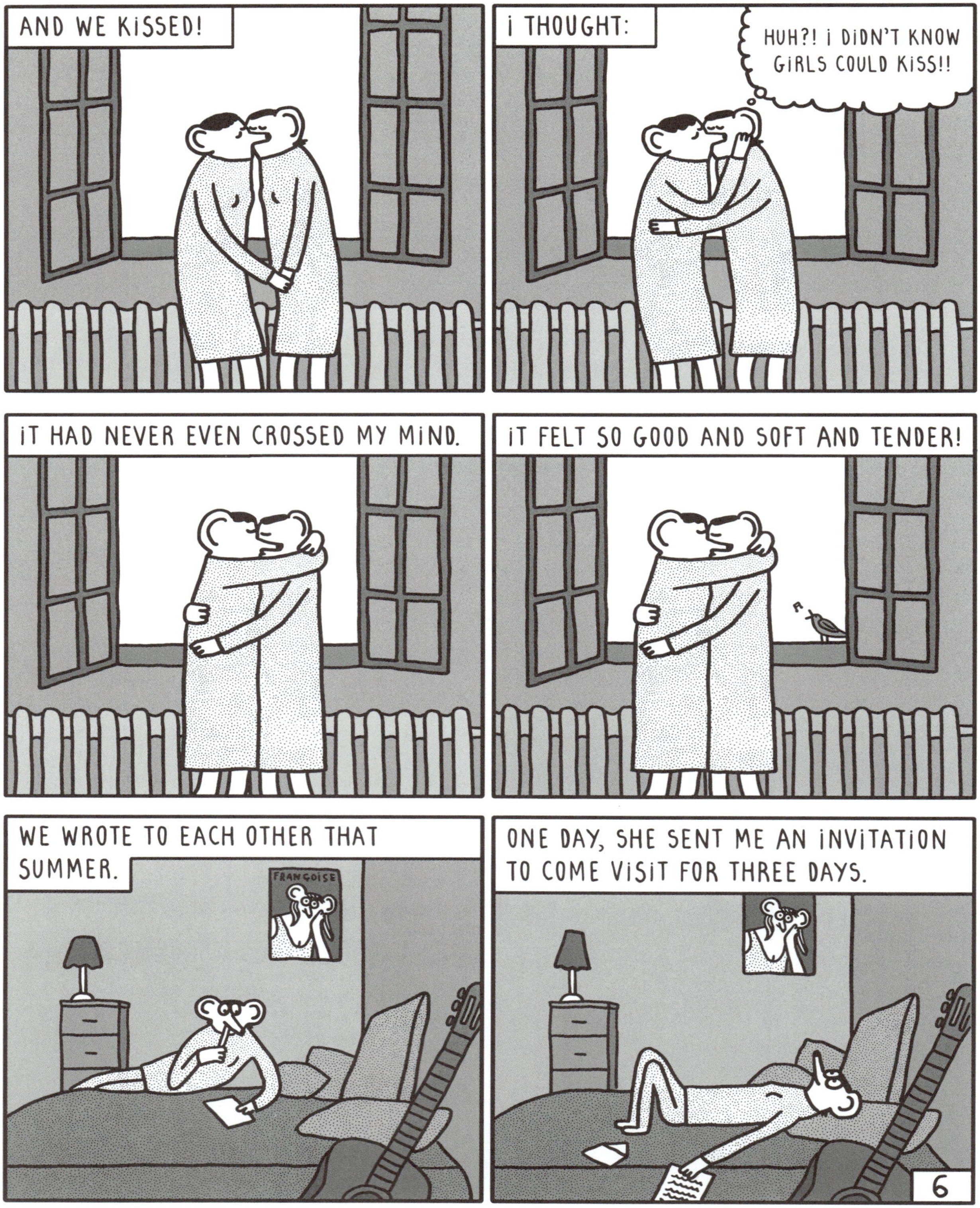
AND WE KISSED!
I THOUGHT:
HUH?! I DIDN'T KNOW GIRLS COULD KISS!!
IT HAD NEVER EVEN CROSSED MY MIND.
IT FELT SO GOOD AND SOFT AND TENDER!
WE WROTE TO EACH OTHER THAT SUMMER.
FRANÇOISE
ONE DAY, SHE SENT ME AN INVITATION TO COME VISIT FOR THREE DAYS.

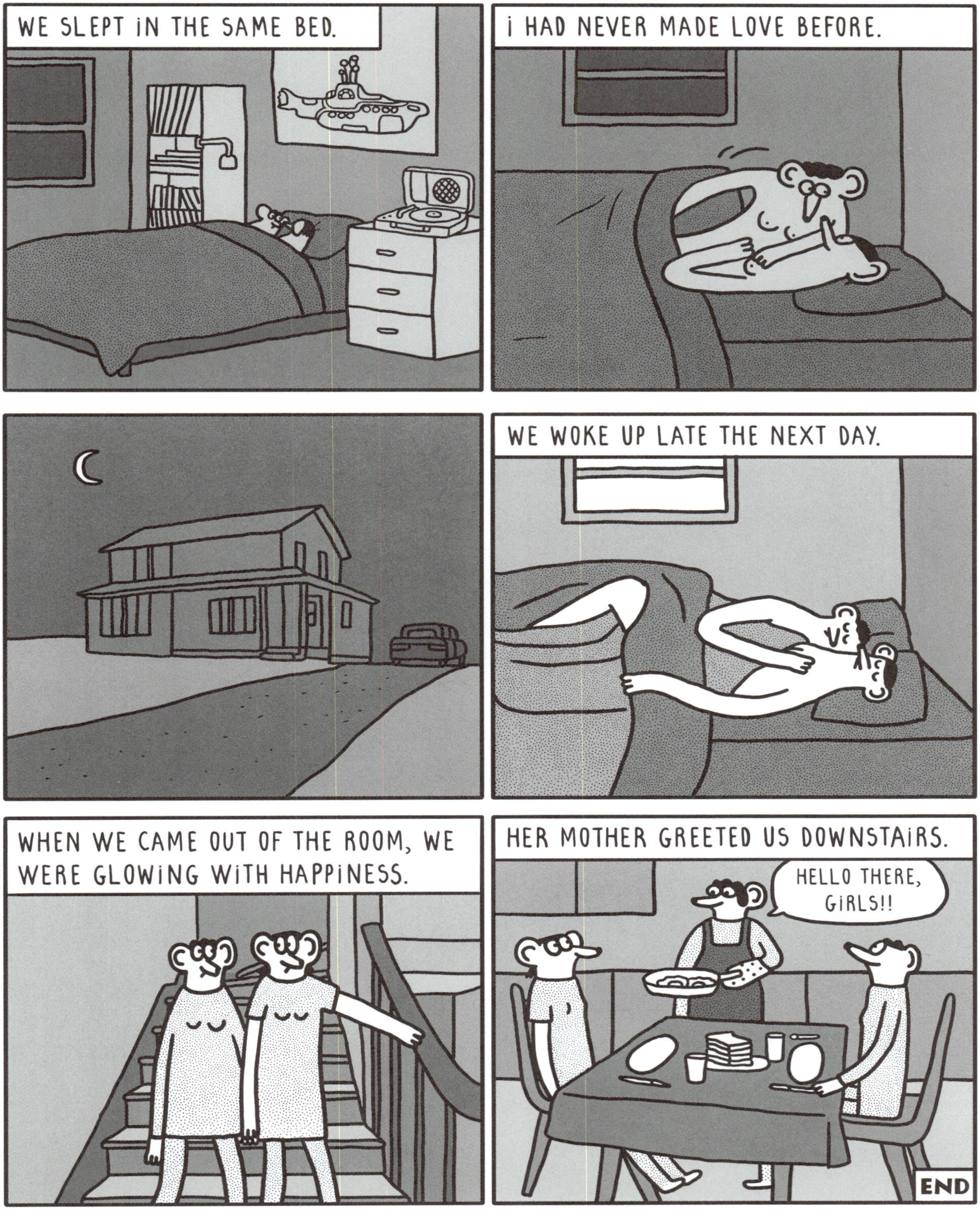
WE SLEPT iN THE SAME BED.
i HAD NEVER MADE LOVE BEFORE.
WE WOKE UP LATE THE NEXT DAY.
WHEN WE CAME OUT OF THE ROOM, WE WERE GLOWiNG WiTH HAPPiNESS.
HER MOTHER GREETED US DOWNSTAiRS.
HELLO THERE, GiRLS!!
END

OCTOBER'S STORY

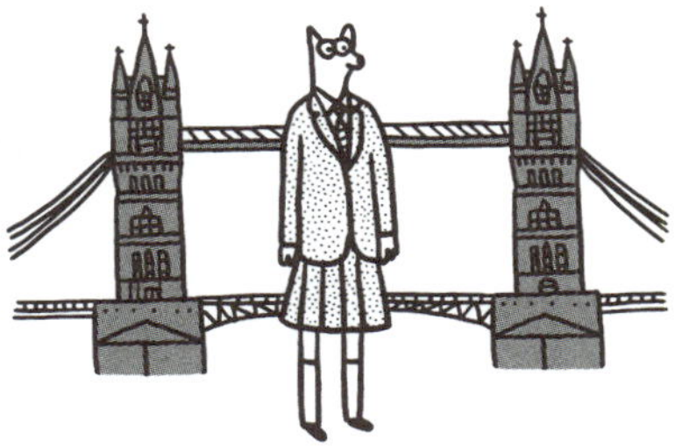

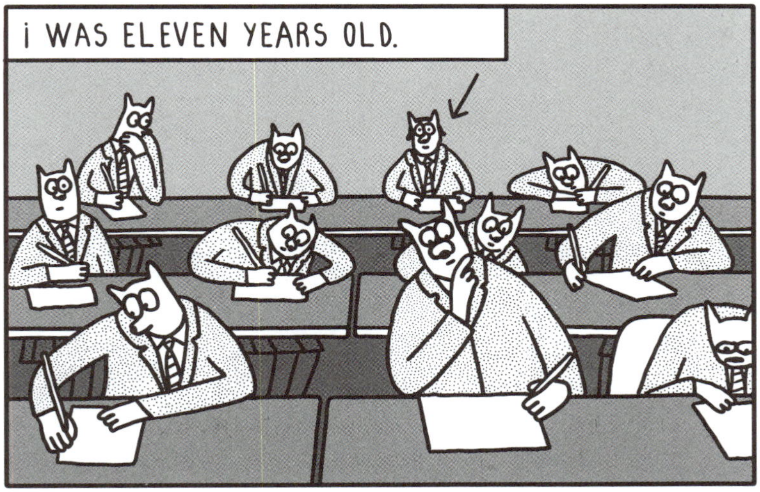

i WAS ELEVEN YEARS OLD.

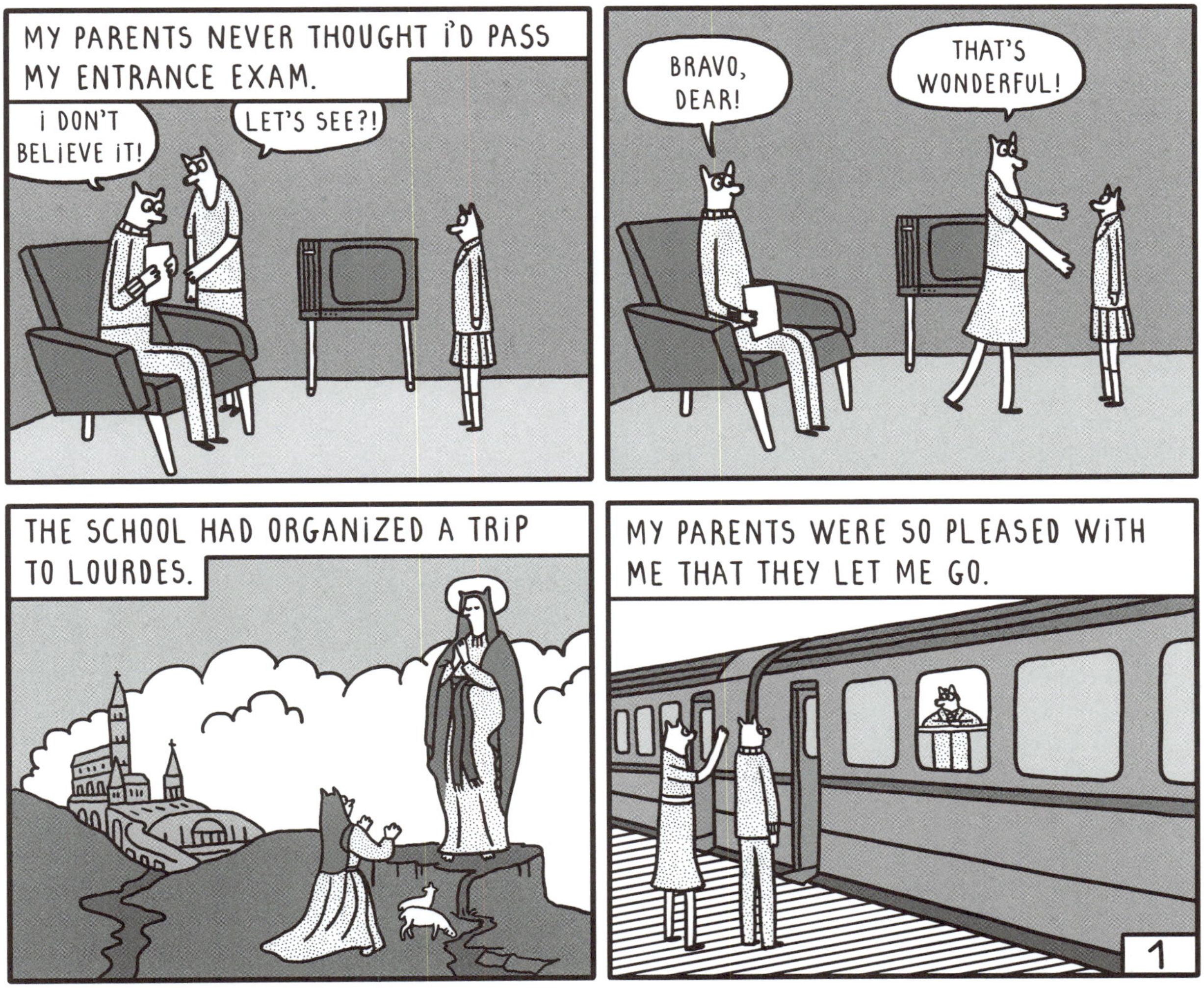

MY PARENTS NEVER THOUGHT i'D PASS MY ENTRANCE EXAM.
i DON'T BELiEVE iT!
LET'S SEE?!
BRAVO, DEAR!
THAT'S WONDERFUL!
THE SCHOOL HAD ORGANiZED A TRiP TO LOURDES.
MY PARENTS WERE SO PLEASED WiTH ME THAT THEY LET ME GO.

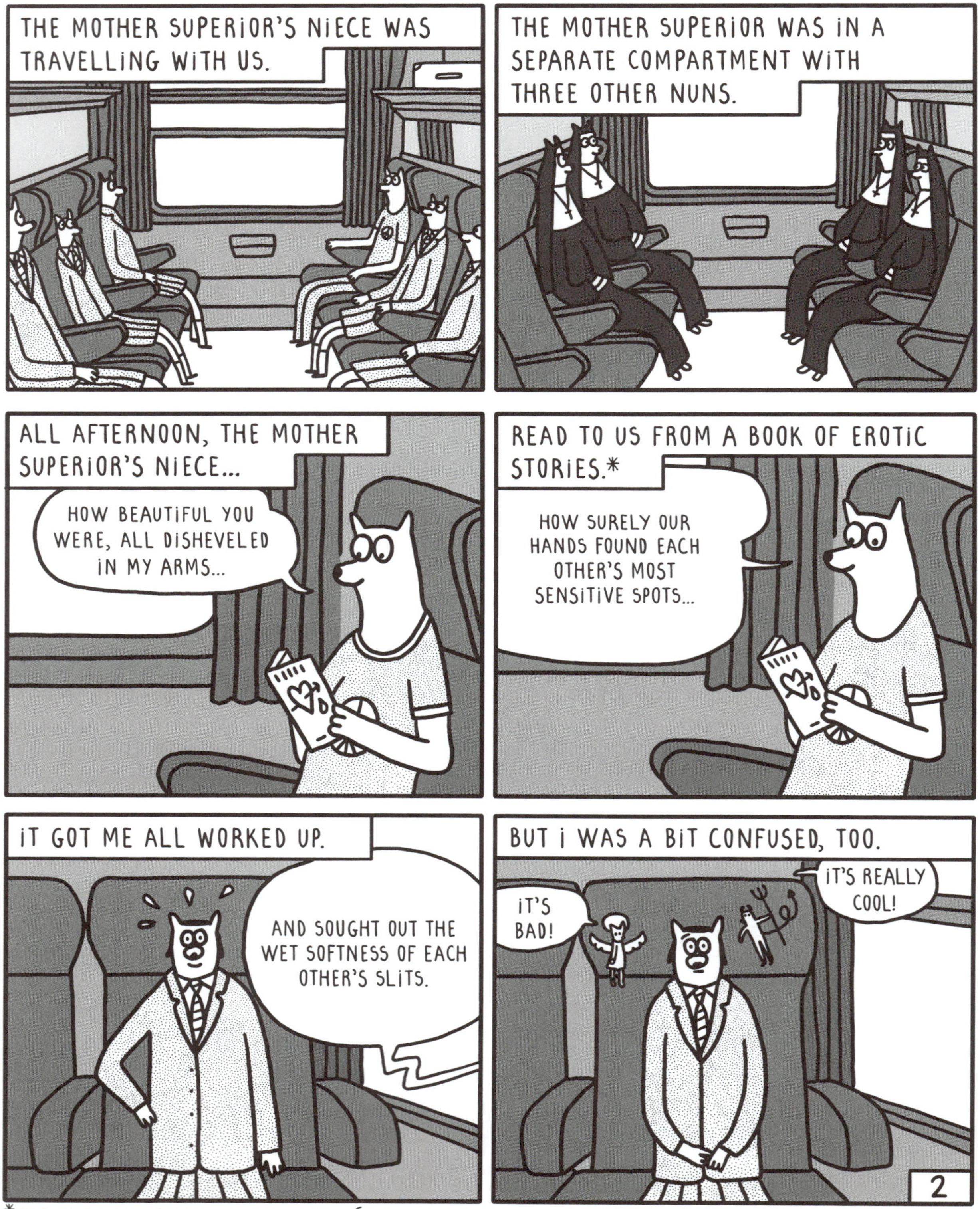
THE MOTHER SUPERIOR'S NIECE WAS TRAVELLING WITH US.
THE MOTHER SUPERIOR WAS IN A SEPARATE COMPARTMENT WITH THREE OTHER NUNS.
ALL AFTERNOON, THE MOTHER SUPERIOR'S NIECE...
HOW BEAUTIFUL YOU WERE, ALL DISHEVELED IN MY ARMS...
READ TO US FROM A BOOK OF EROTIC STORIES.*
HOW SURELY OUR HANDS FOUND EACH OTHER'S MOST SENSITIVE SPOTS...
IT GOT ME ALL WORKED UP.
AND SOUGHT OUT THE WET SOFTNESS OF EACH OTHER'S SLITS.
BUT I WAS A BIT CONFUSED, TOO.
IT'S BAD!
IT'S REALLY COOL!
2

*FOR THE LOVE OF MARIE SALAT BY RÉGINE DEFORGES.

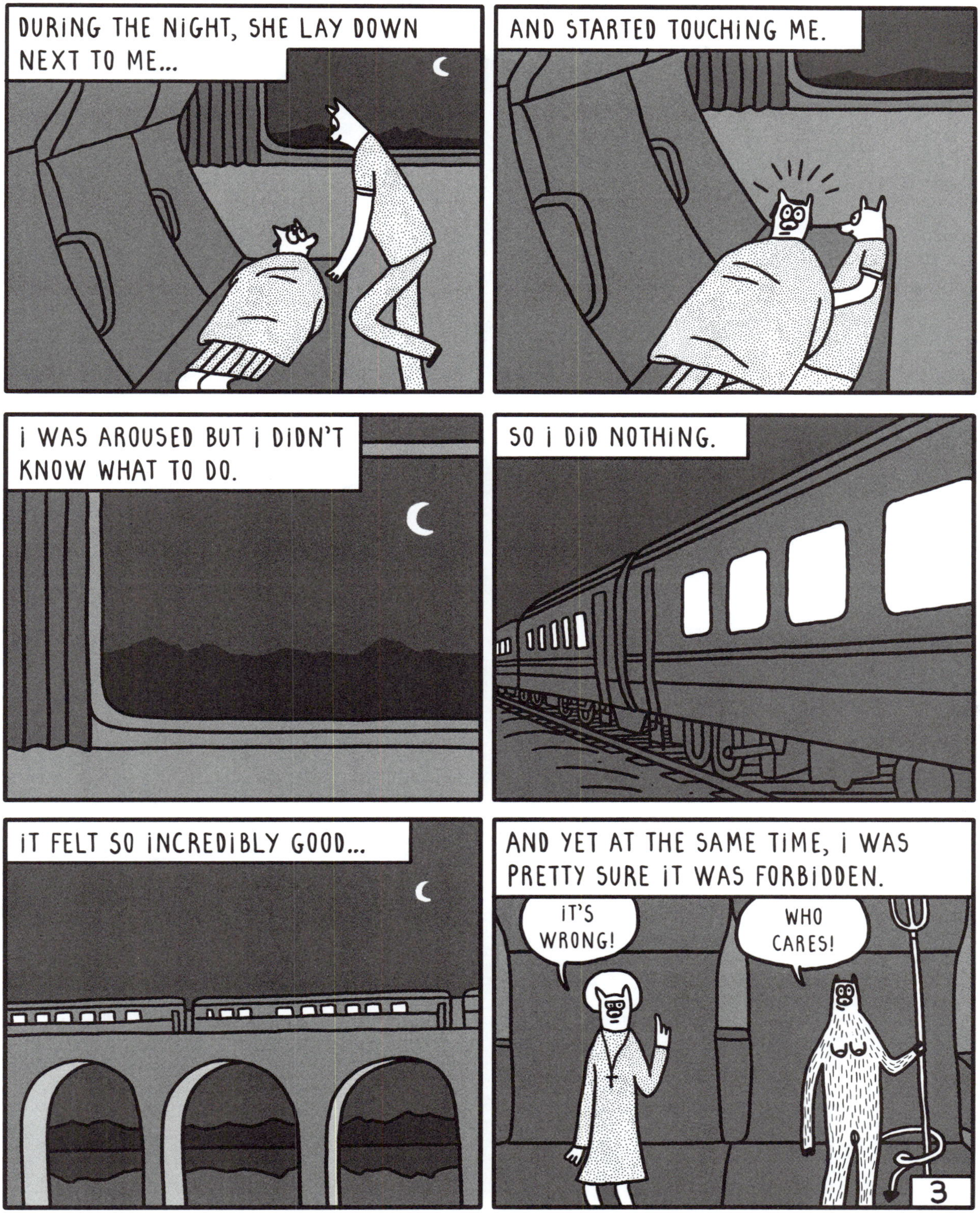
DURING THE NIGHT, SHE LAY DOWN NEXT TO ME...
AND STARTED TOUCHING ME.
I WAS AROUSED BUT I DIDN'T KNOW WHAT TO DO.
SO I DID NOTHING.
IT FELT SO INCREDIBLY GOOD...
AND YET AT THE SAME TIME, I WAS PRETTY SURE IT WAS FORBIDDEN.
IT'S WRONG!
WHO CARES!

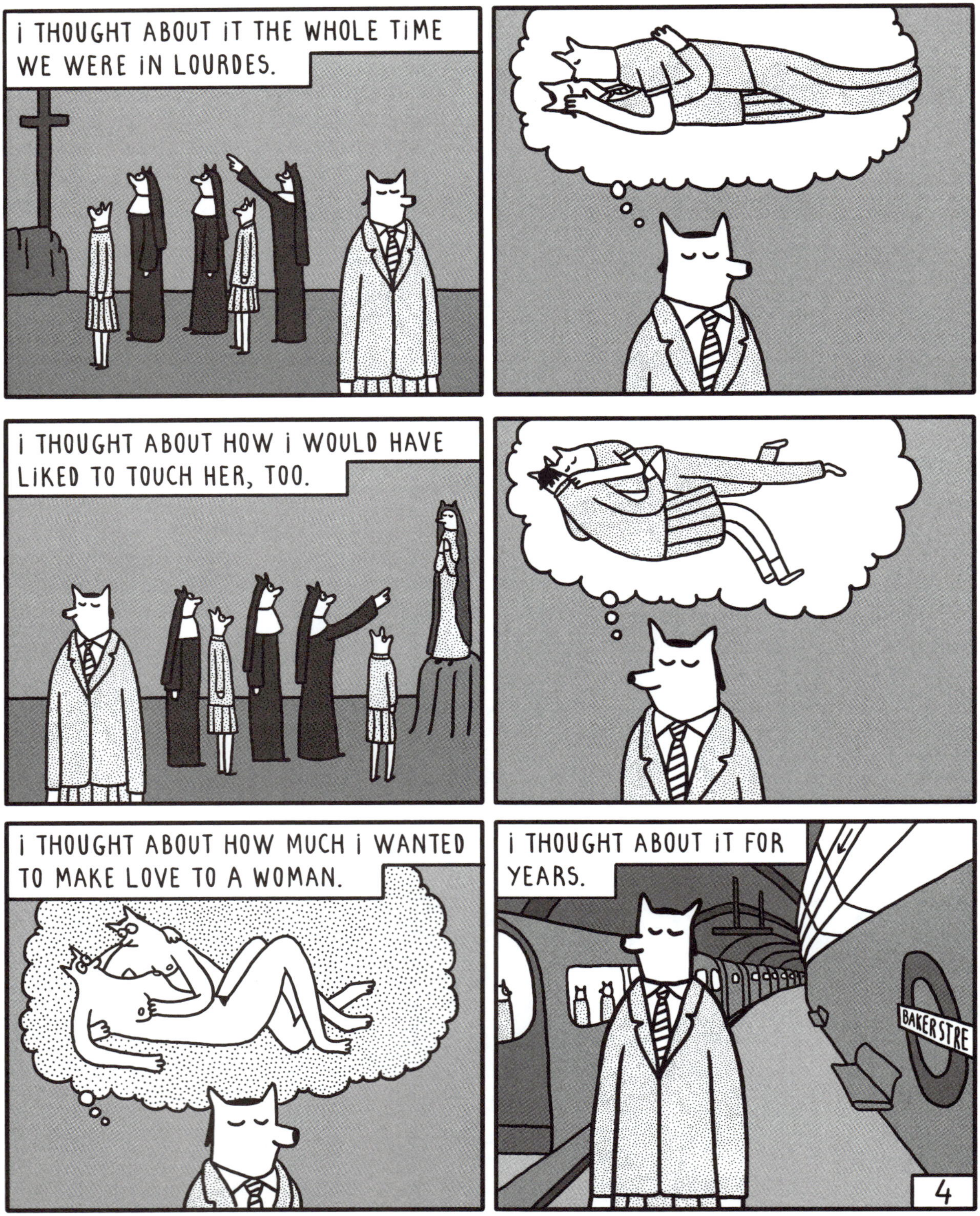
I THOUGHT ABOUT IT THE WHOLE TIME WE WERE IN LOURDES.
I THOUGHT ABOUT HOW I WOULD HAVE LIKED TO TOUCH HER, TOO.
I THOUGHT ABOUT HOW MUCH I WANTED TO MAKE LOVE TO A WOMAN.
I THOUGHT ABOUT IT FOR YEARS.
BAKER STRE

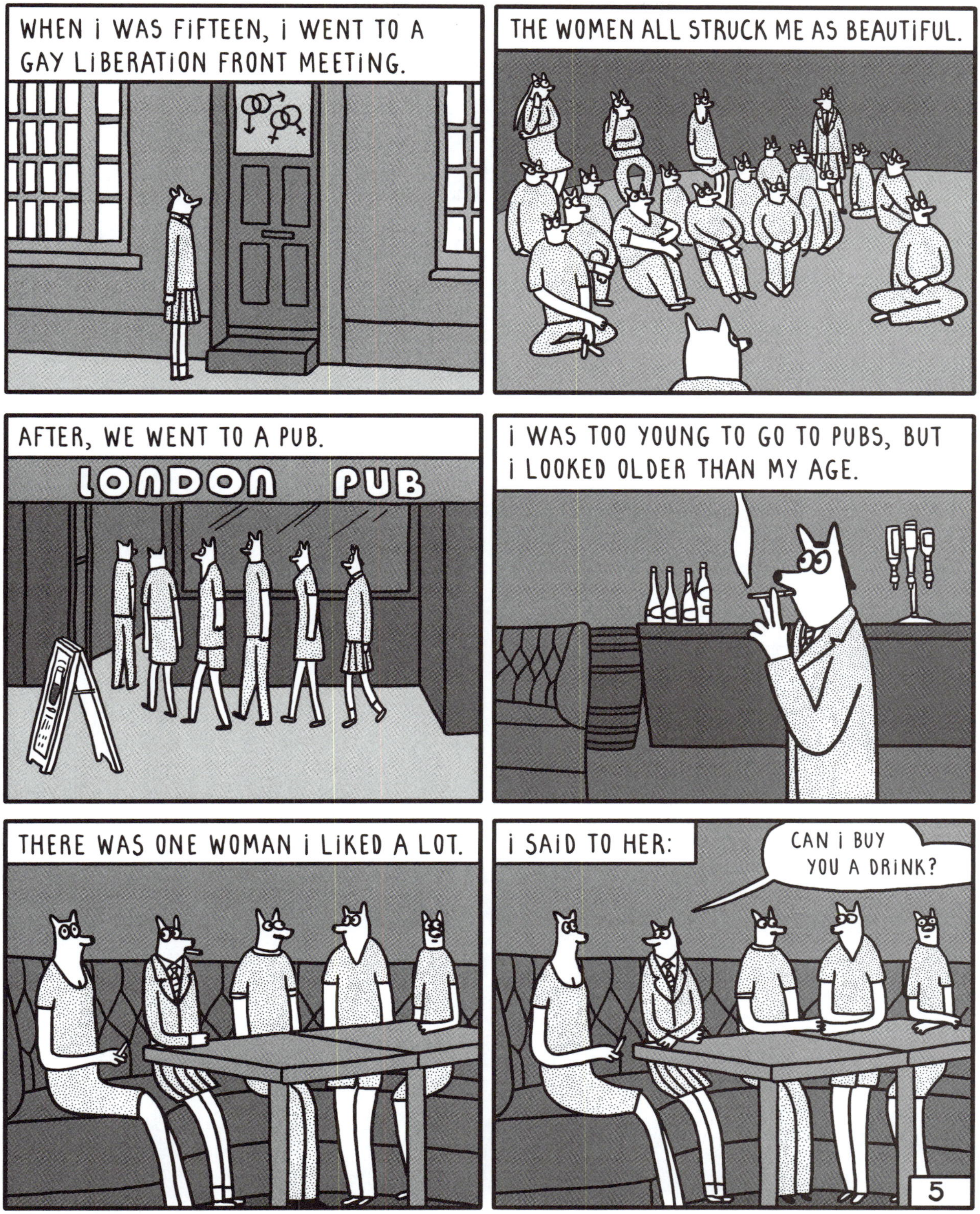
WHEN i WAS FIFTEEN, i WENT TO A GAY LIBERATION FRONT MEETING.
THE WOMEN ALL STRUCK ME AS BEAUTIFUL.
AFTER, WE WENT TO A PUB.
LONDON PUB
i WAS TOO YOUNG TO GO TO PUBS, BUT i LOOKED OLDER THAN MY AGE.
THERE WAS ONE WOMAN i LIKED A LOT.
i SAID TO HER:
CAN i BUY YOU A DRINK?

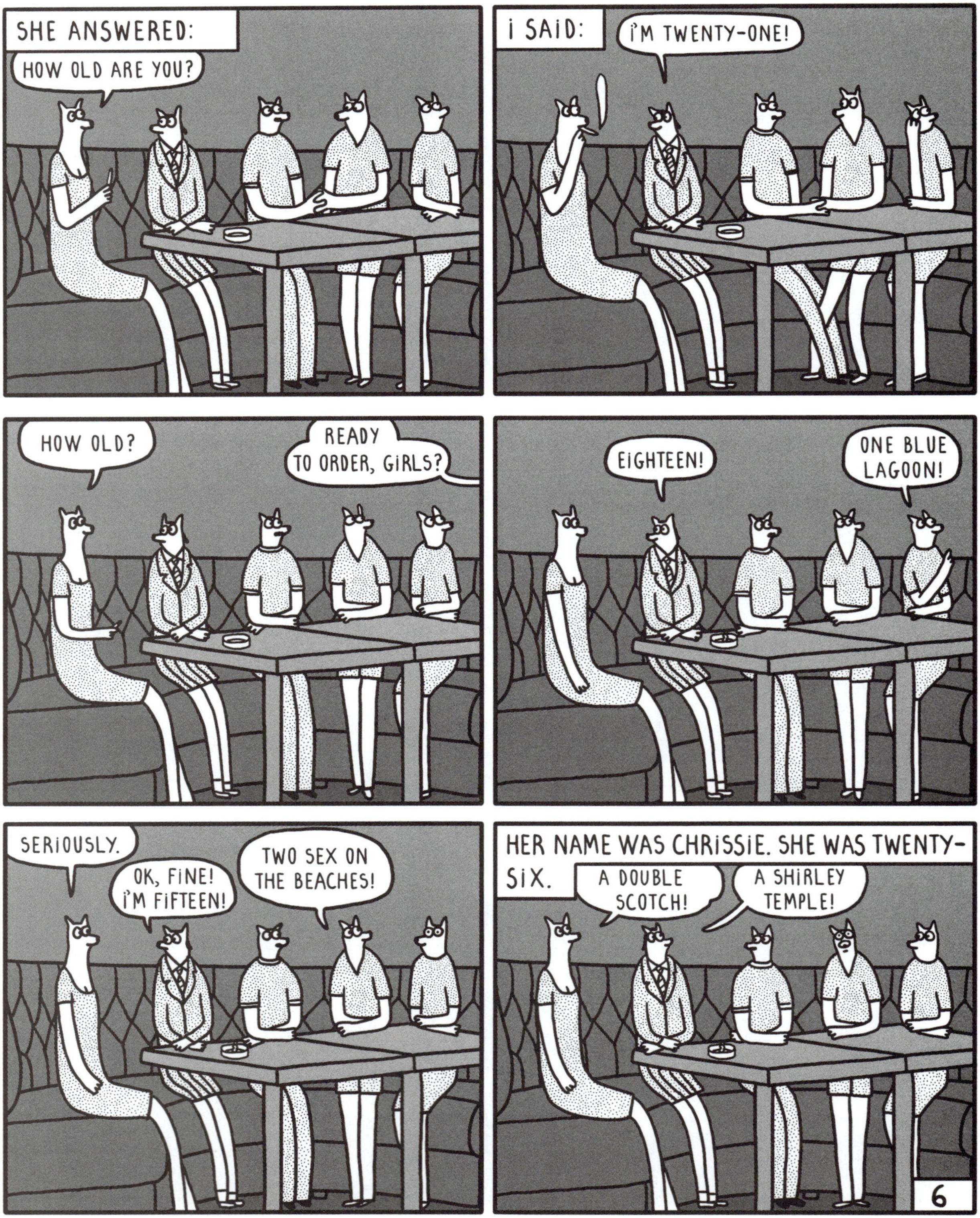
SHE ANSWERED:
HOW OLD ARE YOU?
I SAID:
I'M TWENTY-ONE!
HOW OLD?
READY TO ORDER, GIRLS?
EIGHTEEN!
ONE BLUE LAGOON!
SERIOUSLY.
OK, FINE! I'M FIFTEEN!
TWO SEX ON THE BEACHES!
HER NAME WAS CHRISSIE. SHE WAS TWENTY-SIX.
A DOUBLE SCOTCH!
A SHIRLEY TEMPLE!

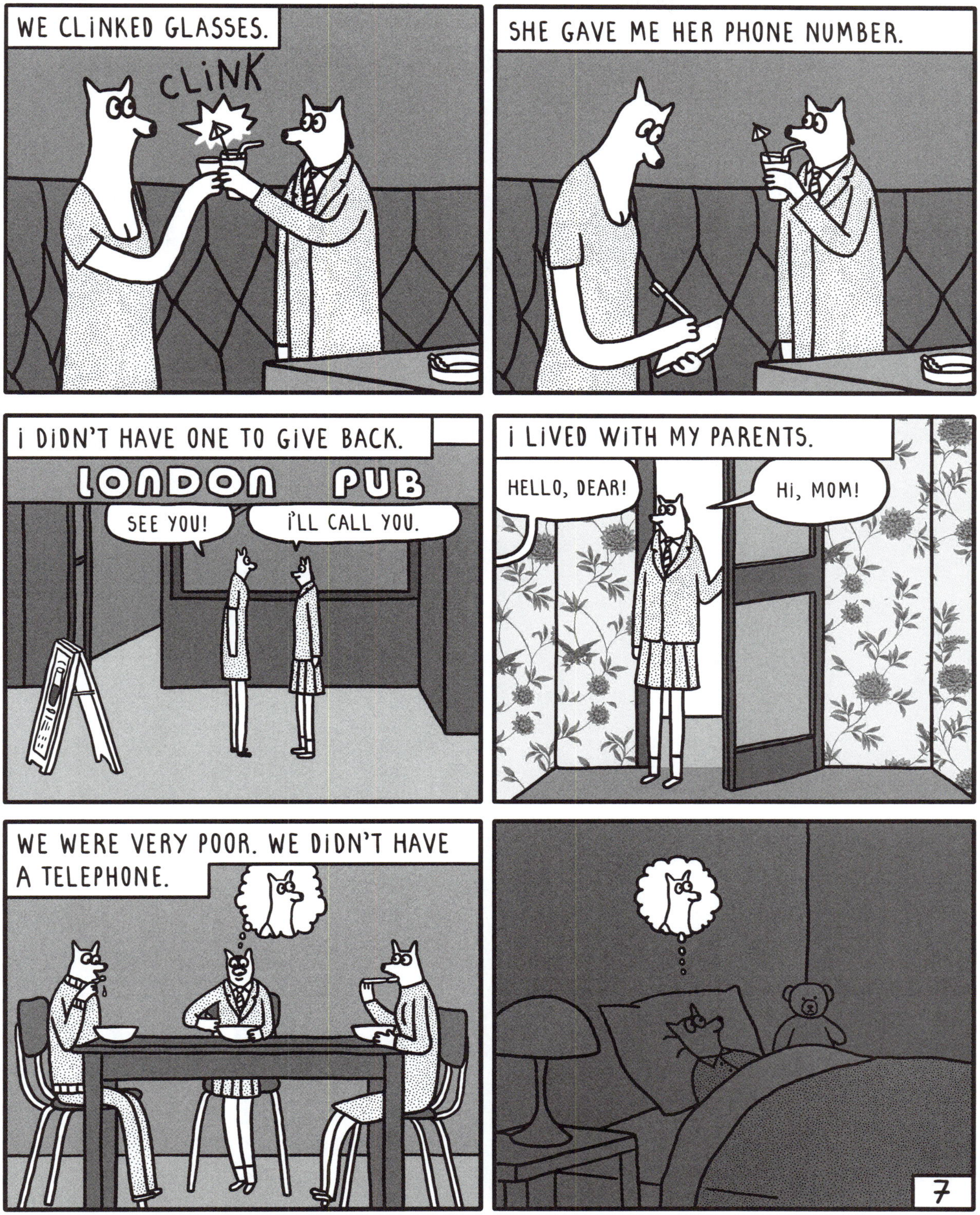
WE CLINKED GLASSES.
CLINK
SHE GAVE ME HER PHONE NUMBER.
I DIDN'T HAVE ONE TO GIVE BACK.
LONDON PUB
SEE YOU!
I'LL CALL YOU.
I LIVED WITH MY PARENTS.
HELLO, DEAR!
HI, MOM!
WE WERE VERY POOR. WE DIDN'T HAVE A TELEPHONE.

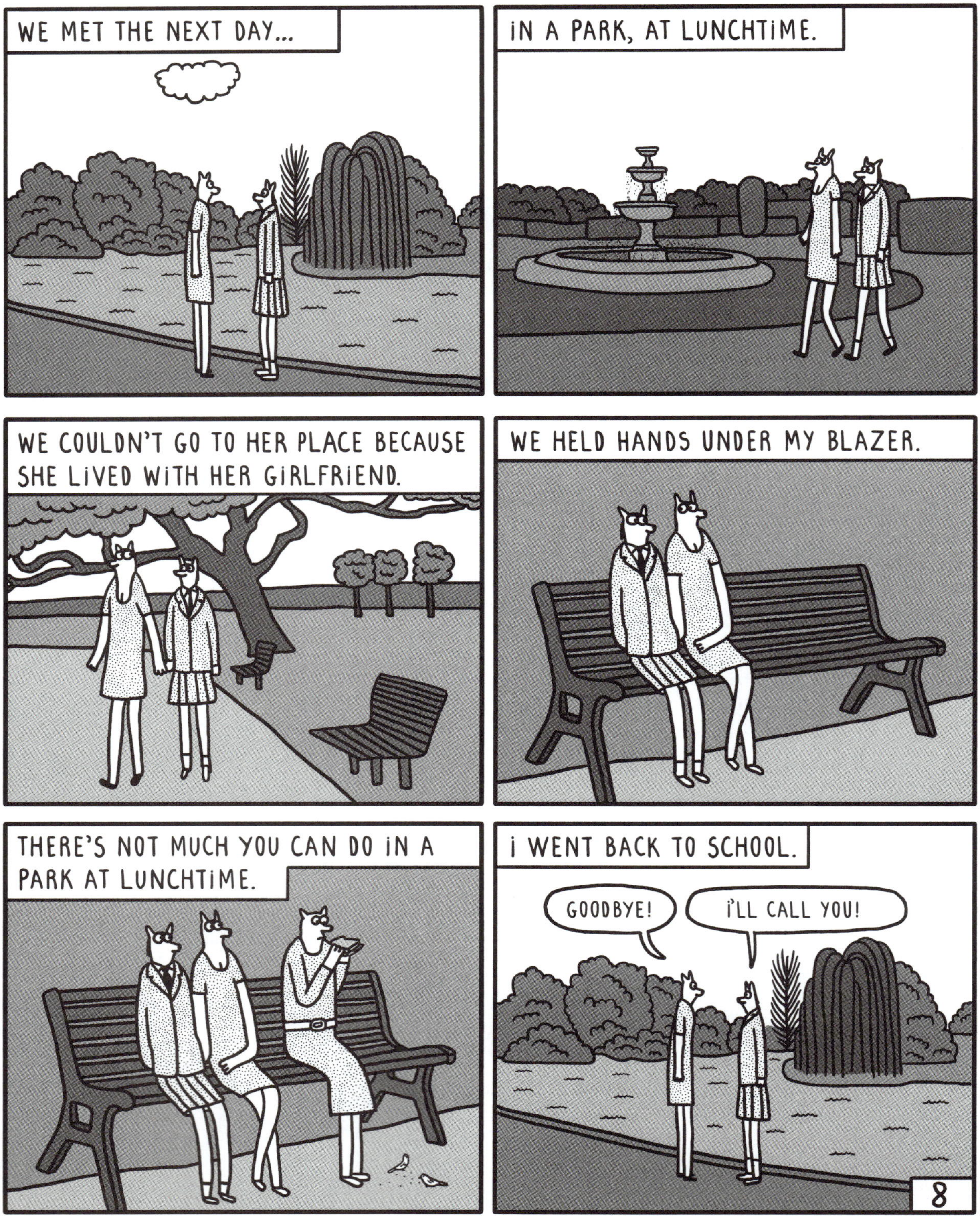
WE MET THE NEXT DAY...
iN A PARK, AT LUNCHTiME.
WE COULDN'T GO TO HER PLACE BECAUSE SHE LiVED WiTH HER GiRLFRiEND.
WE HELD HANDS UNDER MY BLAZER.
THERE'S NOT MUCH YOU CAN DO iN A PARK AT LUNCHTiME.
i WENT BACK TO SCHOOL.
GOODBYE!
i'LL CALL YOU!

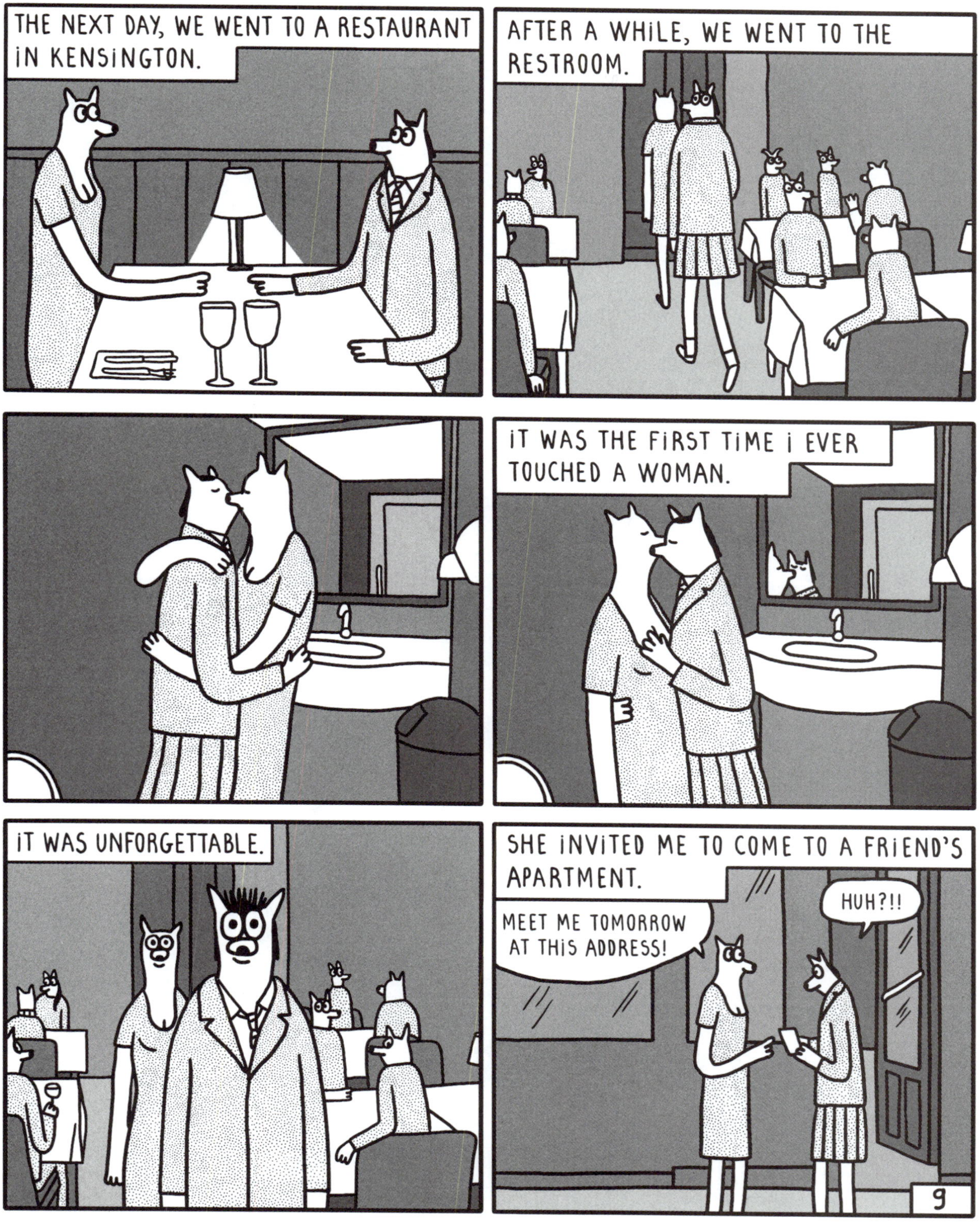
THE NEXT DAY, WE WENT TO A RESTAURANT IN KENSINGTON.
AFTER A WHILE, WE WENT TO THE RESTROOM.
IT WAS THE FIRST TIME I EVER TOUCHED A WOMAN.
IT WAS UNFORGETTABLE.
SHE INVITED ME TO COME TO A FRIEND'S APARTMENT.
MEET ME TOMORROW AT THIS ADDRESS!
HUH?!!
9

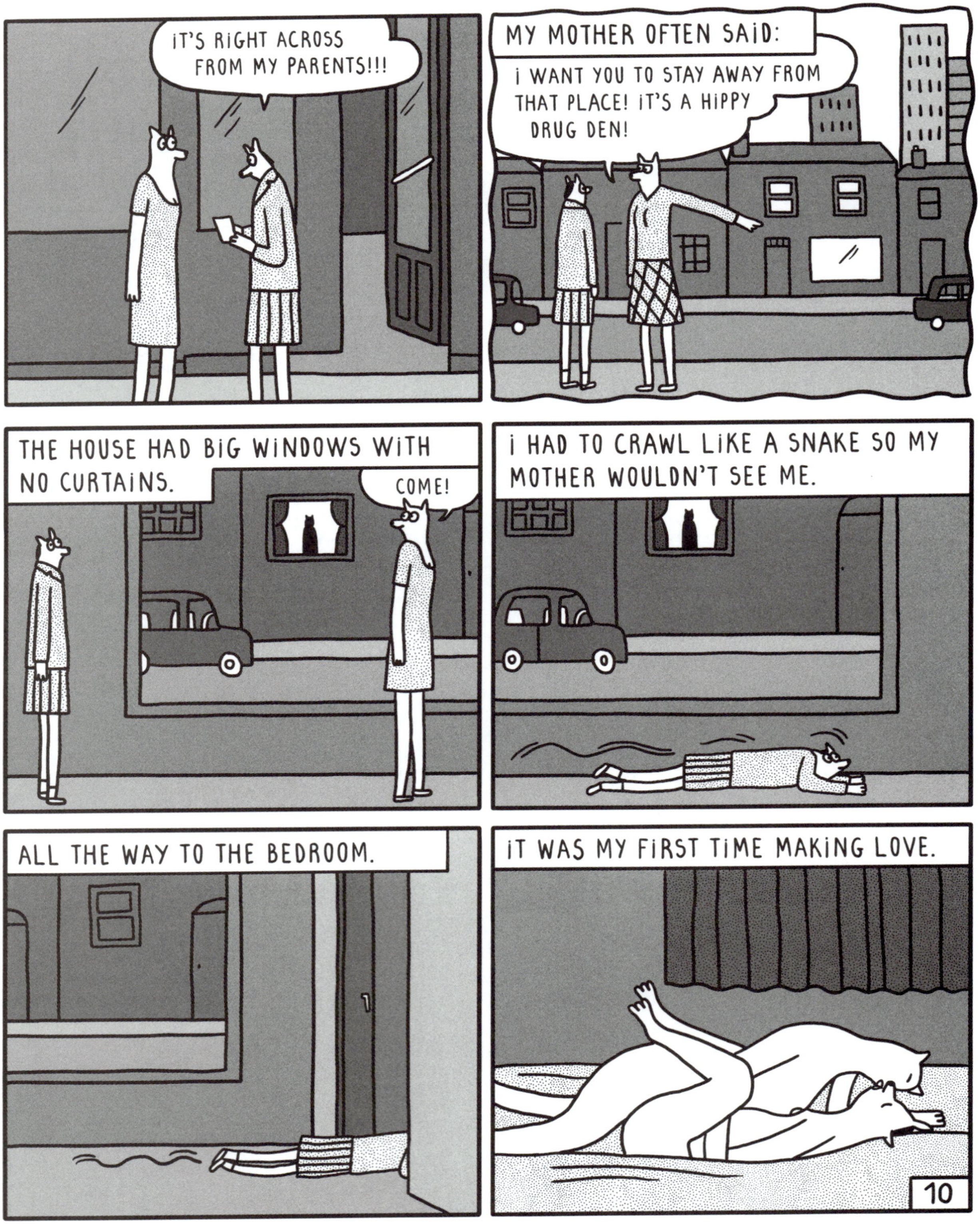
IT'S RIGHT ACROSS FROM MY PARENTS!!!
MY MOTHER OFTEN SAID:
I WANT YOU TO STAY AWAY FROM THAT PLACE! IT'S A HIPPY DRUG DEN!
THE HOUSE HAD BIG WINDOWS WITH NO CURTAINS.
COME!
I HAD TO CRAWL LIKE A SNAKE SO MY MOTHER WOULDN'T SEE ME.
ALL THE WAY TO THE BEDROOM.
IT WAS MY FIRST TIME MAKING LOVE.
10

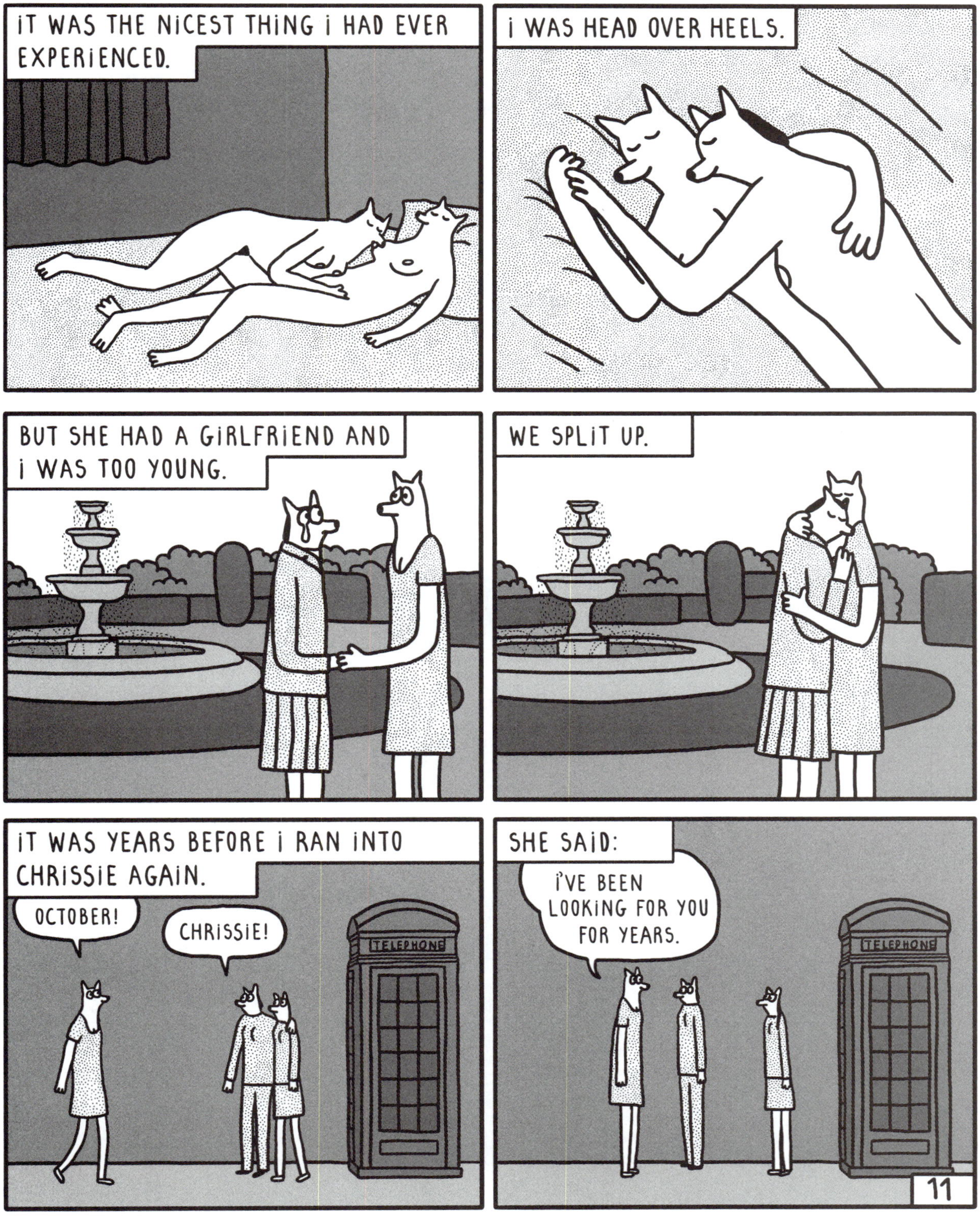
IT WAS THE NICEST THING I HAD EVER EXPERIENCED.
I WAS HEAD OVER HEELS.
BUT SHE HAD A GIRLFRIEND AND I WAS TOO YOUNG.
WE SPLIT UP.
IT WAS YEARS BEFORE I RAN INTO CHRISSIE AGAIN.
OCTOBER!
CHRISSIE!
TELEPHONE
SHE SAID:
I'VE BEEN LOOKING FOR YOU FOR YEARS.
TELEPHONE

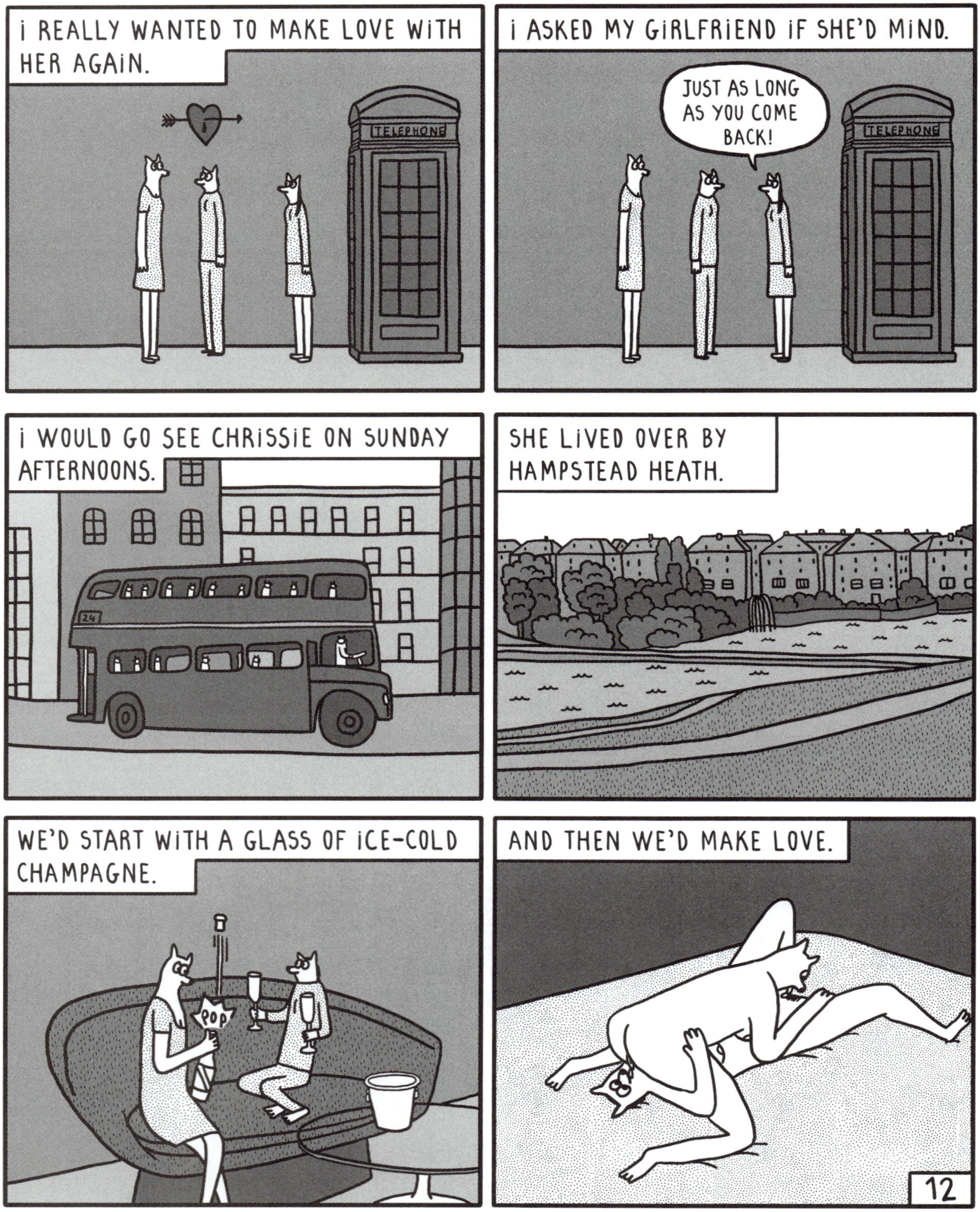

i REALLY WANTED TO MAKE LOVE WiTH HER AGAiN.
TELEPHONE
i ASKED MY GiRLFRiEND iF SHE'D MiND.
JUST AS LONG AS YOU COME BACK!
TELEPHONE
i WOULD GO SEE CHRiSSiE ON SUNDAY AFTERNOONS.
24
SHE LiVED OVER BY HAMPSTEAD HEATH.
WE'D START WiTH A GLASS OF iCE-COLD CHAMPAGNE.
POP
AND THEN WE'D MAKE LOVE.

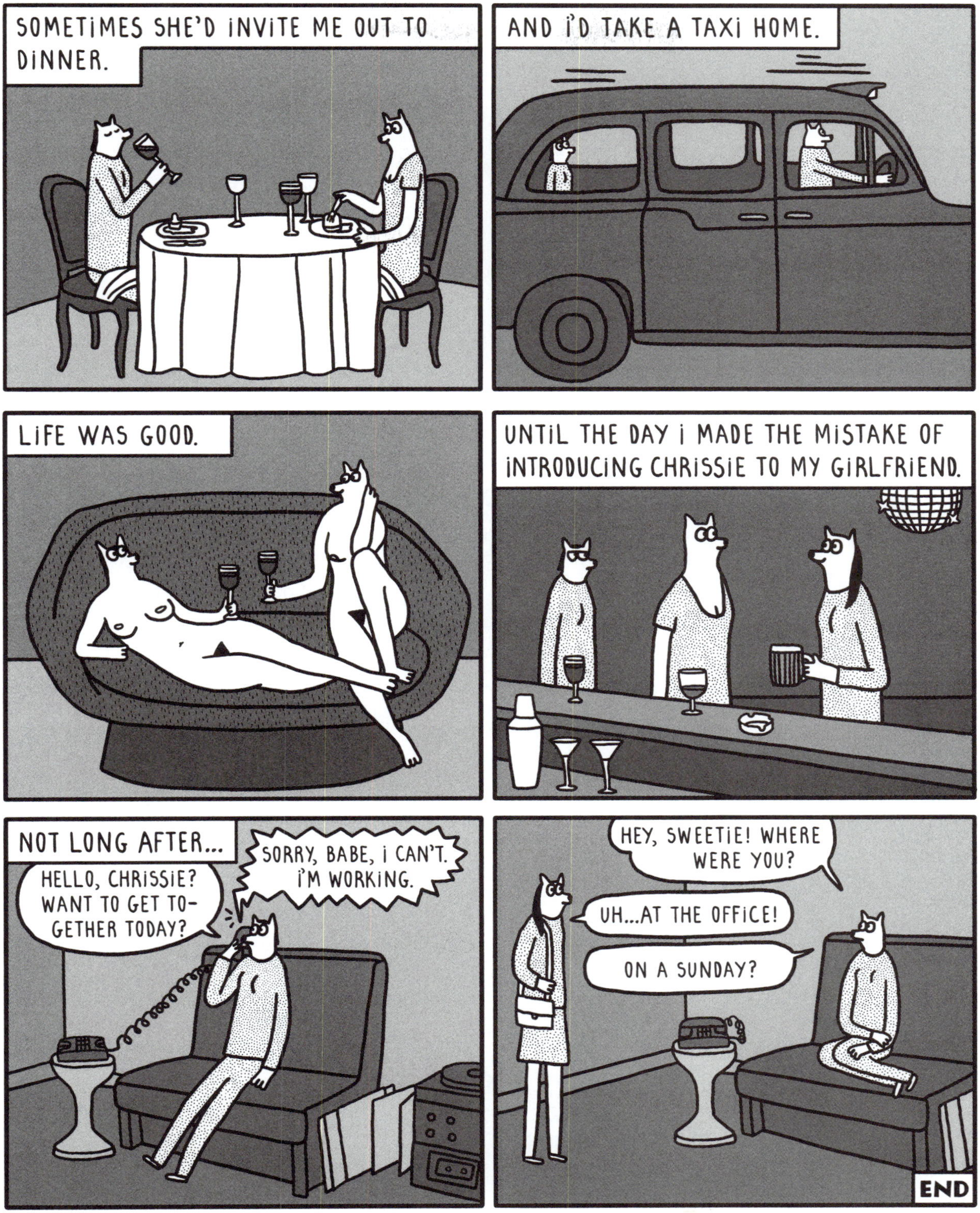
SOMETIMES SHE'D INVITE ME OUT TO DINNER.
AND I'D TAKE A TAXI HOME.
LIFE WAS GOOD.
UNTIL THE DAY I MADE THE MISTAKE OF INTRODUCING CHRISSIE TO MY GIRLFRIEND.
NOT LONG AFTER...
HELLO, CHRISSIE? WANT TO GET TO-GETHER TODAY?
SORRY, BABE, I CAN'T. I'M WORKING.
HEY, SWEETIE! WHERE WERE YOU?
UH...AT THE OFFICE!
ON A SUNDAY?
END

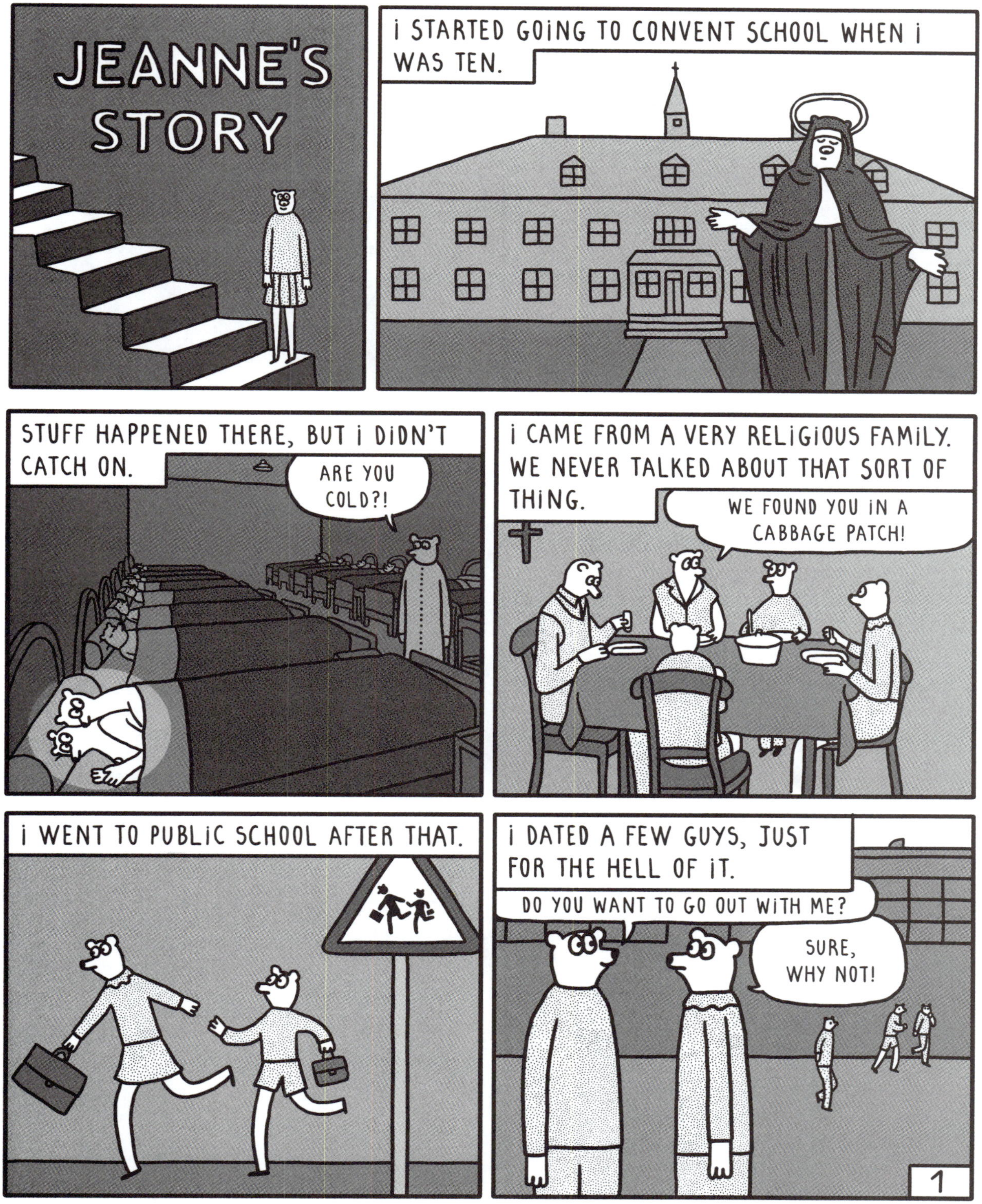
JEANNE'S STORY
i STARTED GOiNG TO CONVENT SCHOOL WHEN i WAS TEN.
STUFF HAPPENED THERE, BUT i DiDN'T CATCH ON.
ARE YOU COLD?!
i CAME FROM A VERY RELiGiOUS FAMiLY. WE NEVER TALKED ABOUT THAT SORT OF THiNG.
WE FOUND YOU iN A CABBAGE PATCH!
i WENT TO PUBLiC SCHOOL AFTER THAT.
i DATED A FEW GUYS, JUST FOR THE HELL OF iT.
DO YOU WANT TO GO OUT WiTH ME?
SURE, WHY NOT!
1

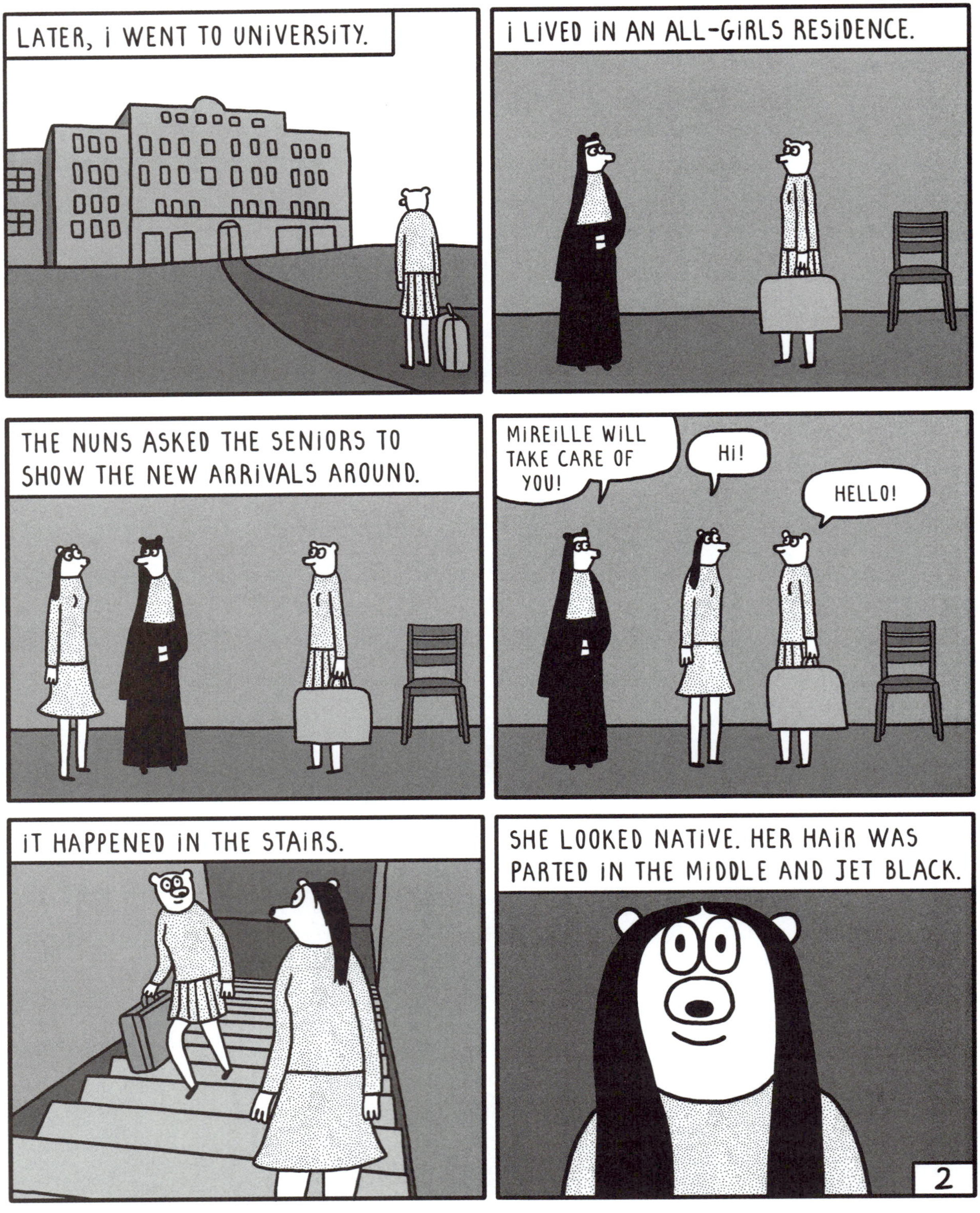
LATER, I WENT TO UNIVERSITY.
I LIVED IN AN ALL-GIRLS RESIDENCE.
THE NUNS ASKED THE SENIORS TO SHOW THE NEW ARRIVALS AROUND.
MIREILLE WILL TAKE CARE OF YOU!
HI!
HELLO!
IT HAPPENED IN THE STAIRS.
SHE LOOKED NATIVE. HER HAIR WAS PARTED IN THE MIDDLE AND JET BLACK.

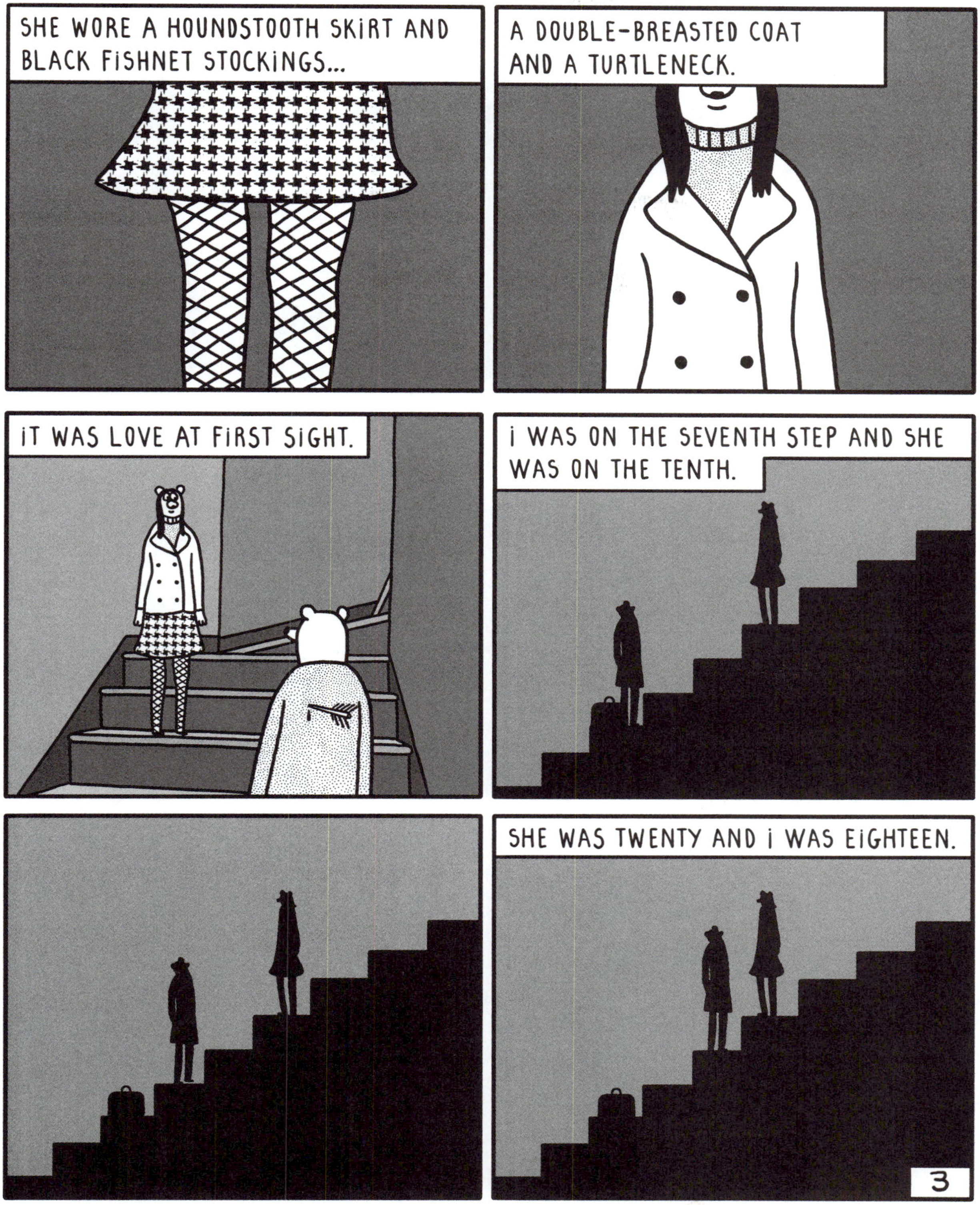
SHE WORE A HOUNDSTOOTH SKIRT AND BLACK FISHNET STOCKINGS...
A DOUBLE-BREASTED COAT AND A TURTLENECK.
IT WAS LOVE AT FIRST SIGHT.
I WAS ON THE SEVENTH STEP AND SHE WAS ON THE TENTH.
SHE WAS TWENTY AND I WAS EIGHTEEN.

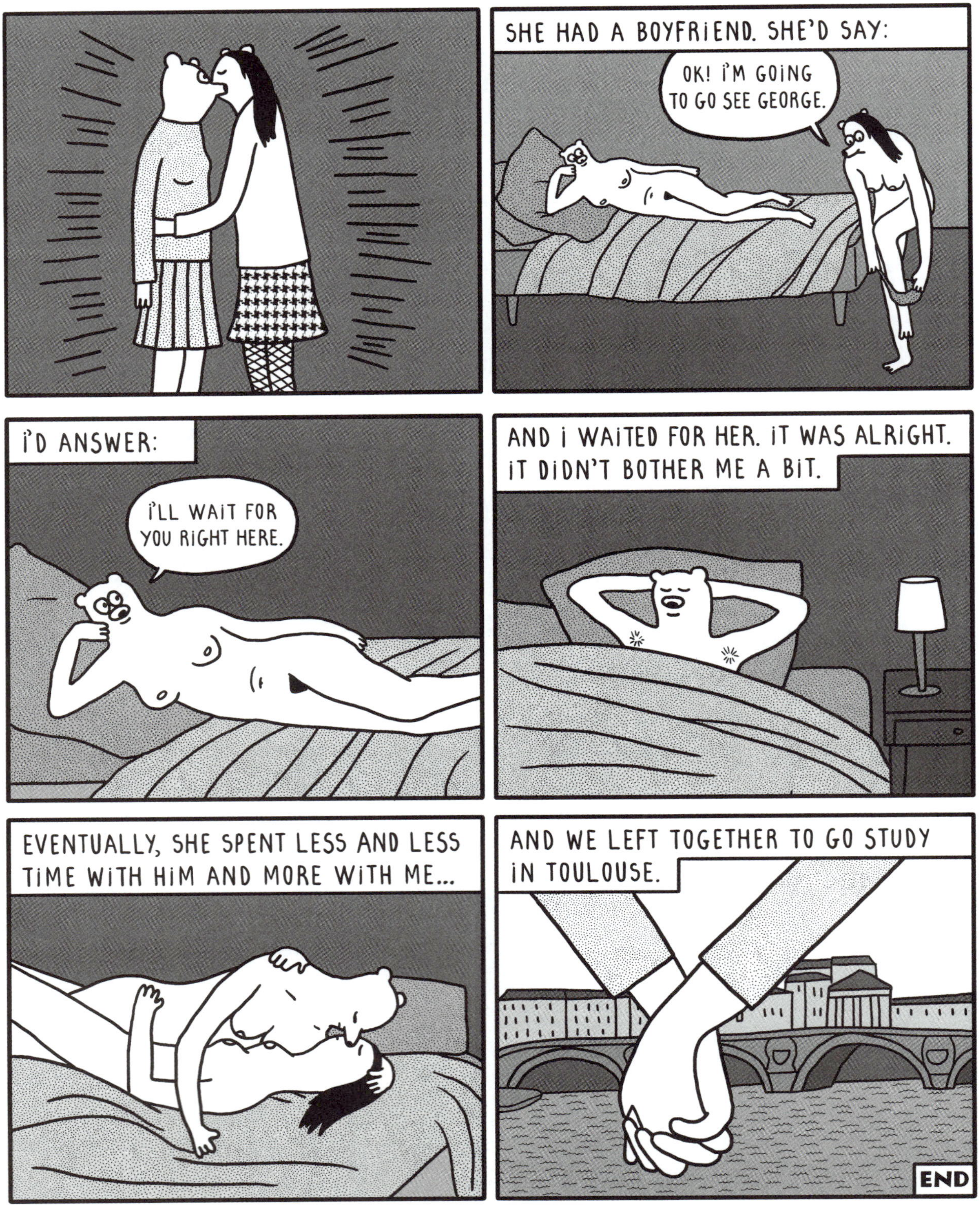
SHE HAD A BOYFRIEND. SHE'D SAY:
OK! I'M GOING TO GO SEE GEORGE.
I'D ANSWER:
I'LL WAIT FOR YOU RIGHT HERE.
AND I WAITED FOR HER. IT WAS ALRIGHT. IT DIDN'T BOTHER ME A BIT.
EVENTUALLY, SHE SPENT LESS AND LESS TIME WITH HIM AND MORE WITH ME...
AND WE LEFT TOGETHER TO GO STUDY IN TOULOUSE.
END

M-H'S STORY

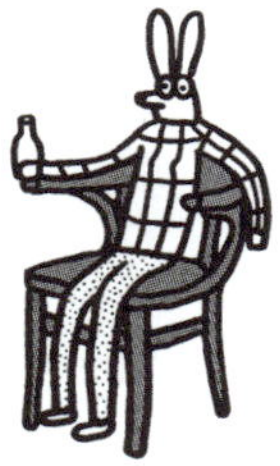

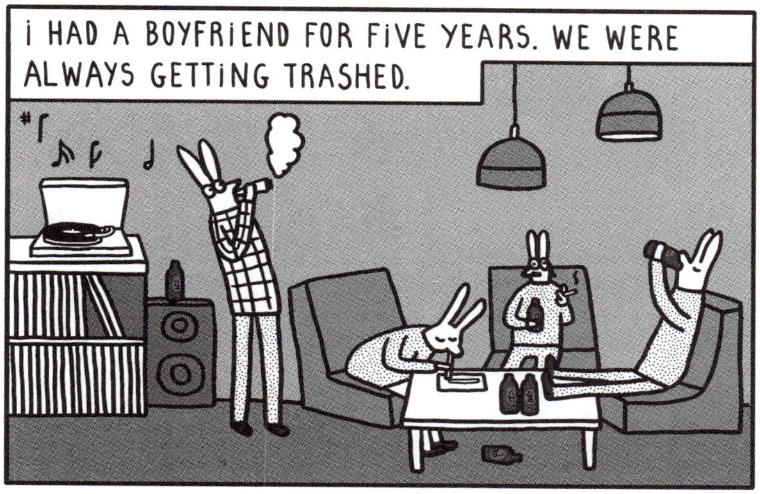
I HAD A BOYFRIEND FOR FIVE YEARS. WE WERE ALWAYS GETTING TRASHED.

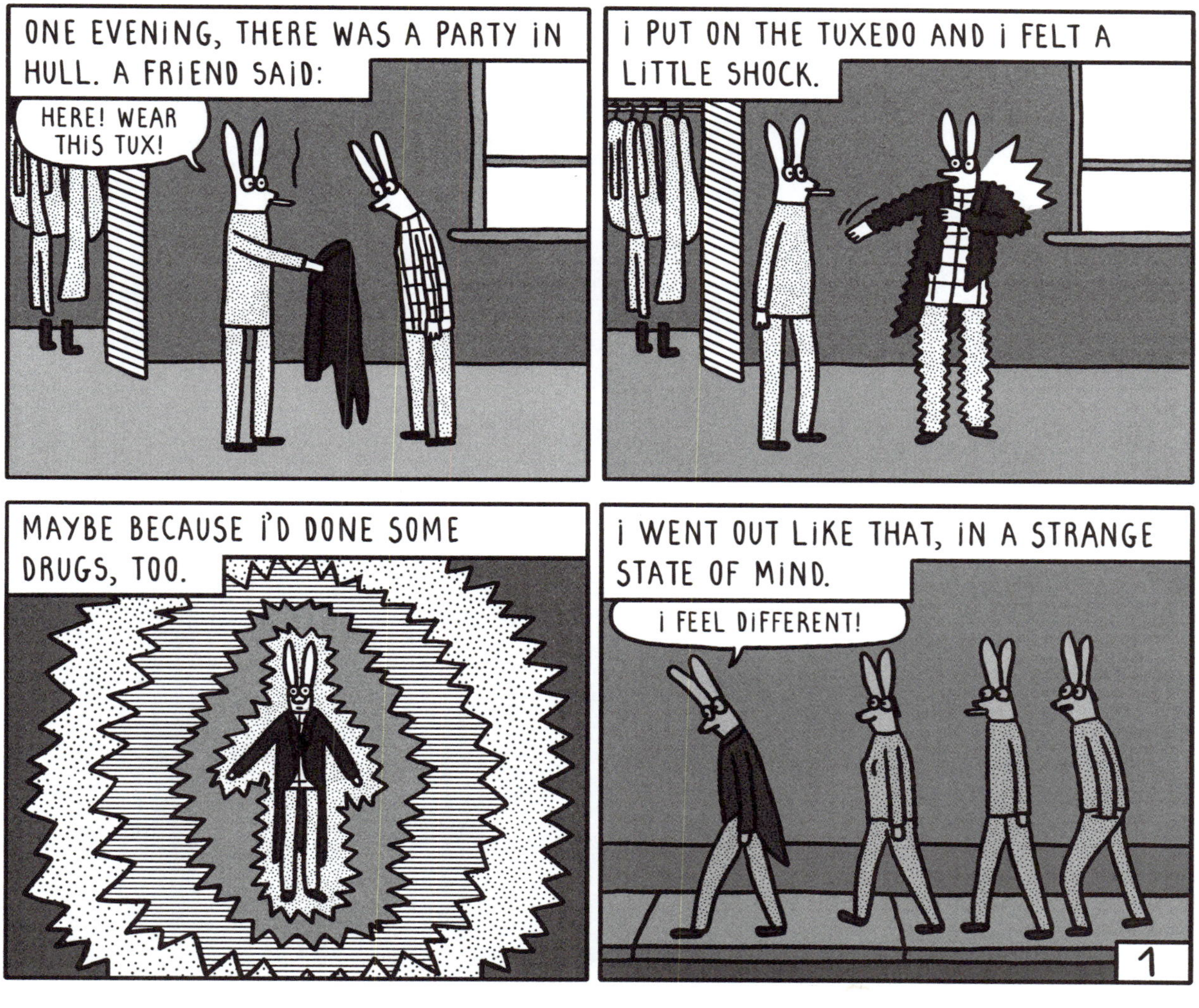
ONE EVENING, THERE WAS A PARTY IN HULL. A FRIEND SAID:
HERE! WEAR THIS TUX!
I PUT ON THE TUXEDO AND I FELT A LITTLE SHOCK.
MAYBE BECAUSE I'D DONE SOME DRUGS, TOO.
I WENT OUT LIKE THAT, IN A STRANGE STATE OF MIND.
I FEEL DIFFERENT!

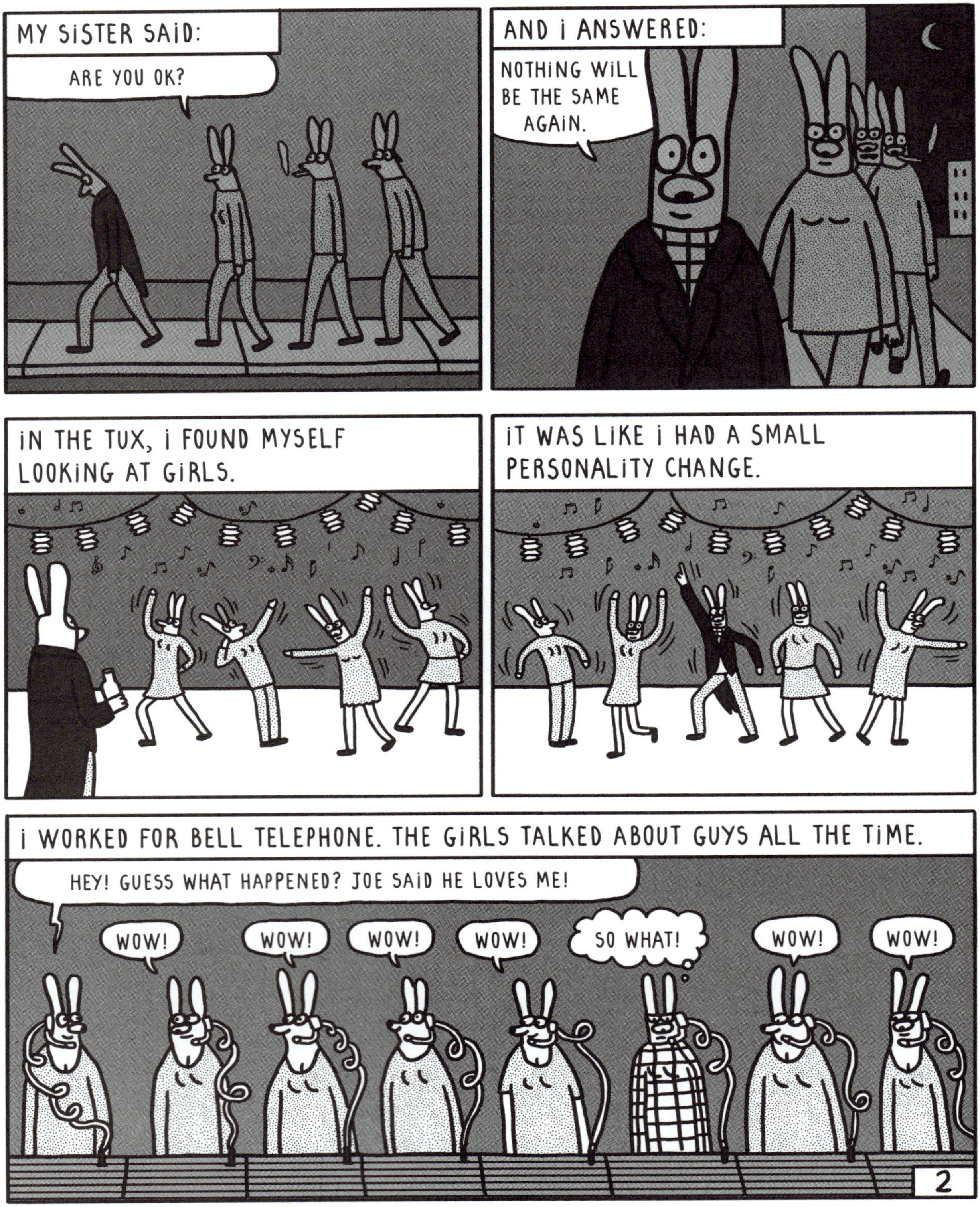

MY SISTER SAID:
ARE YOU OK?
AND I ANSWERED:
NOTHING WILL BE THE SAME AGAIN.
IN THE TUX, I FOUND MYSELF LOOKING AT GIRLS.
IT WAS LIKE I HAD A SMALL PERSONALITY CHANGE.
I WORKED FOR BELL TELEPHONE. THE GIRLS TALKED ABOUT GUYS ALL THE TIME.
HEY! GUESS WHAT HAPPENED? JOE SAID HE LOVES ME!
WOW!
WOW!
WOW!
WOW!
SO WHAT!
WOW!
WOW!

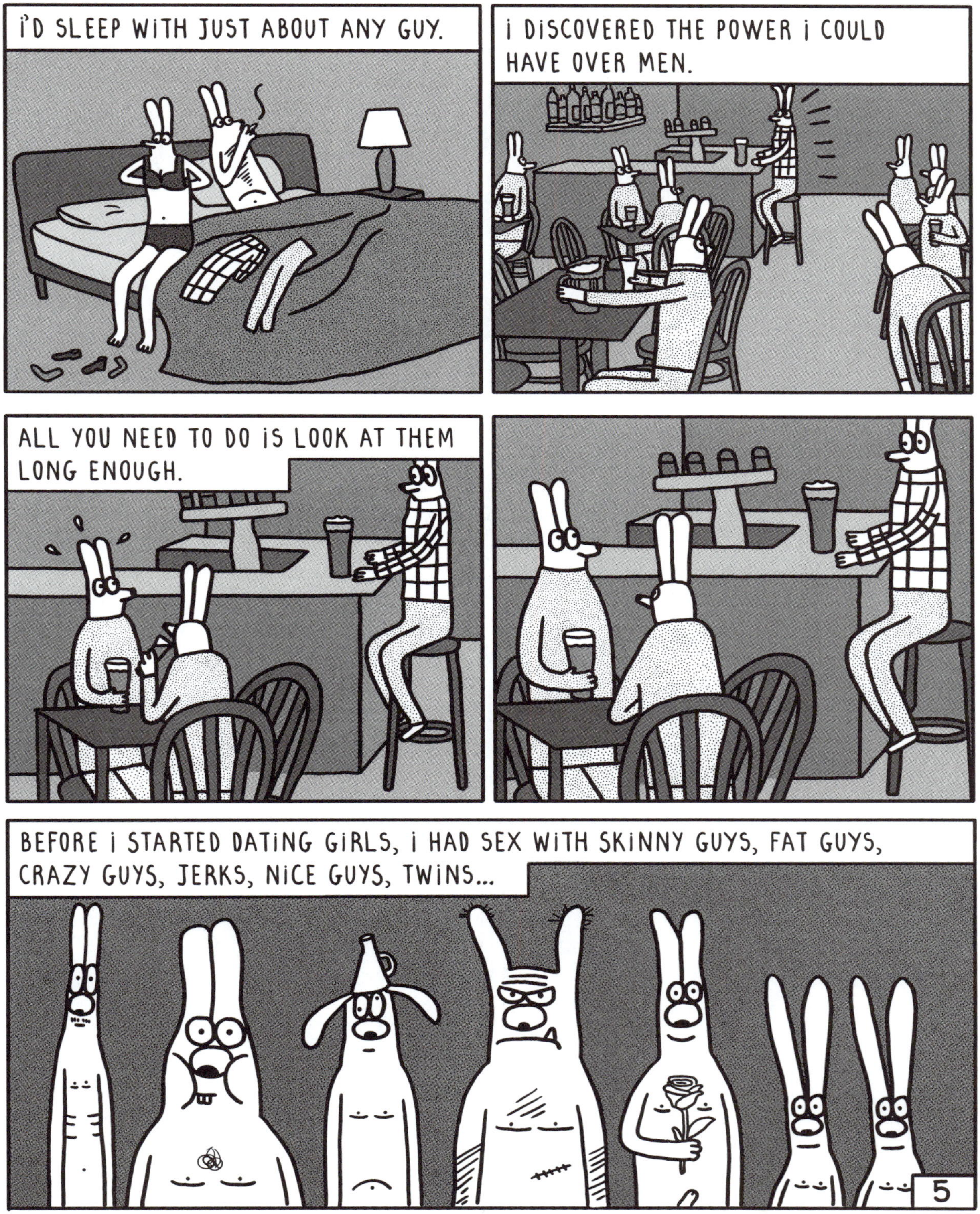
I'D SLEEP WITH JUST ABOUT ANY GUY.
I DISCOVERED THE POWER I COULD HAVE OVER MEN.
ALL YOU NEED TO DO IS LOOK AT THEM LONG ENOUGH.
BEFORE I STARTED DATING GIRLS, I HAD SEX WITH SKINNY GUYS, FAT GUYS, CRAZY GUYS, JERKS, NICE GUYS, TWINS...

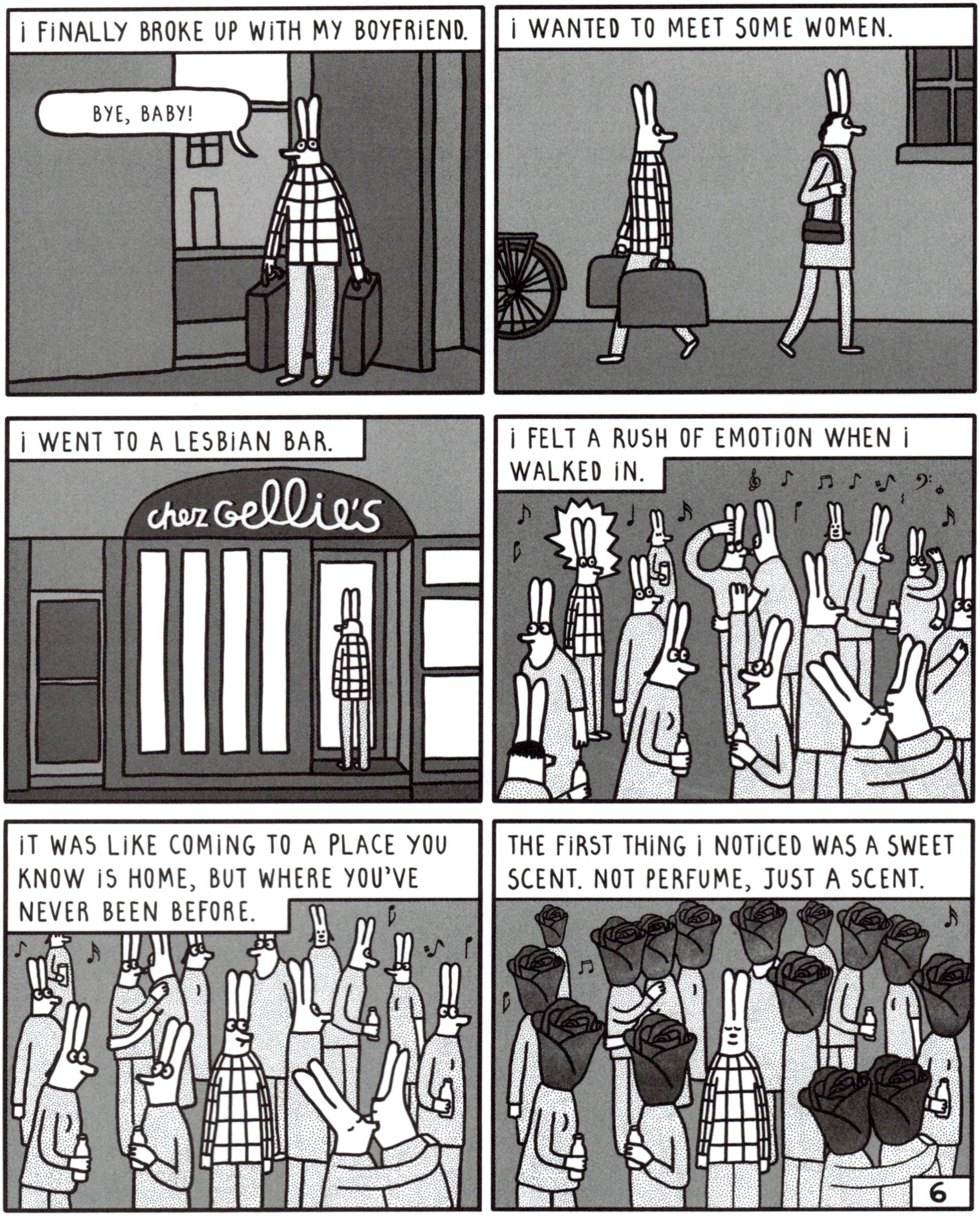

i FINALLY BROKE UP WITH MY BOYFRIEND.
BYE, BABY!
i WANTED TO MEET SOME WOMEN.
i WENT TO A LESBIAN BAR.
chez gellie's
i FELT A RUSH OF EMOTION WHEN i WALKED iN.
iT WAS LIKE COMiNG TO A PLACE YOU KNOW iS HOME, BUT WHERE YOU'VE NEVER BEEN BEFORE.
THE FIRST THiNG i NOTiCED WAS A SWEET SCENT. NOT PERFUME, JUST A SCENT.

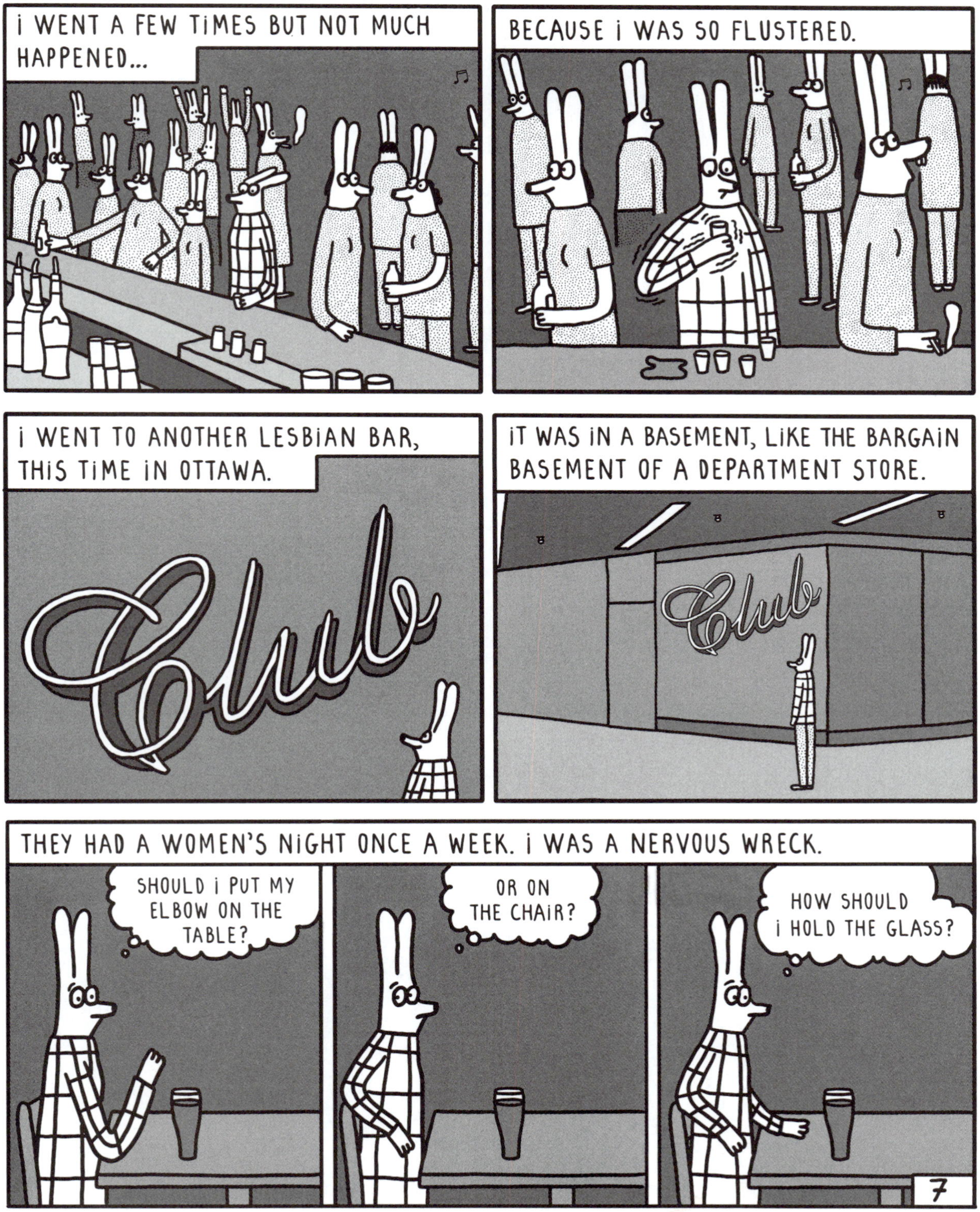
I WENT A FEW TIMES BUT NOT MUCH HAPPENED...
BECAUSE I WAS SO FLUSTERED.
I WENT TO ANOTHER LESBIAN BAR, THIS TIME IN OTTAWA.
Club
IT WAS IN A BASEMENT, LIKE THE BARGAIN BASEMENT OF A DEPARTMENT STORE.
Club
THEY HAD A WOMEN'S NIGHT ONCE A WEEK. I WAS A NERVOUS WRECK.
SHOULD I PUT MY ELBOW ON THE TABLE?
OR ON THE CHAIR?
HOW SHOULD I HOLD THE GLASS?

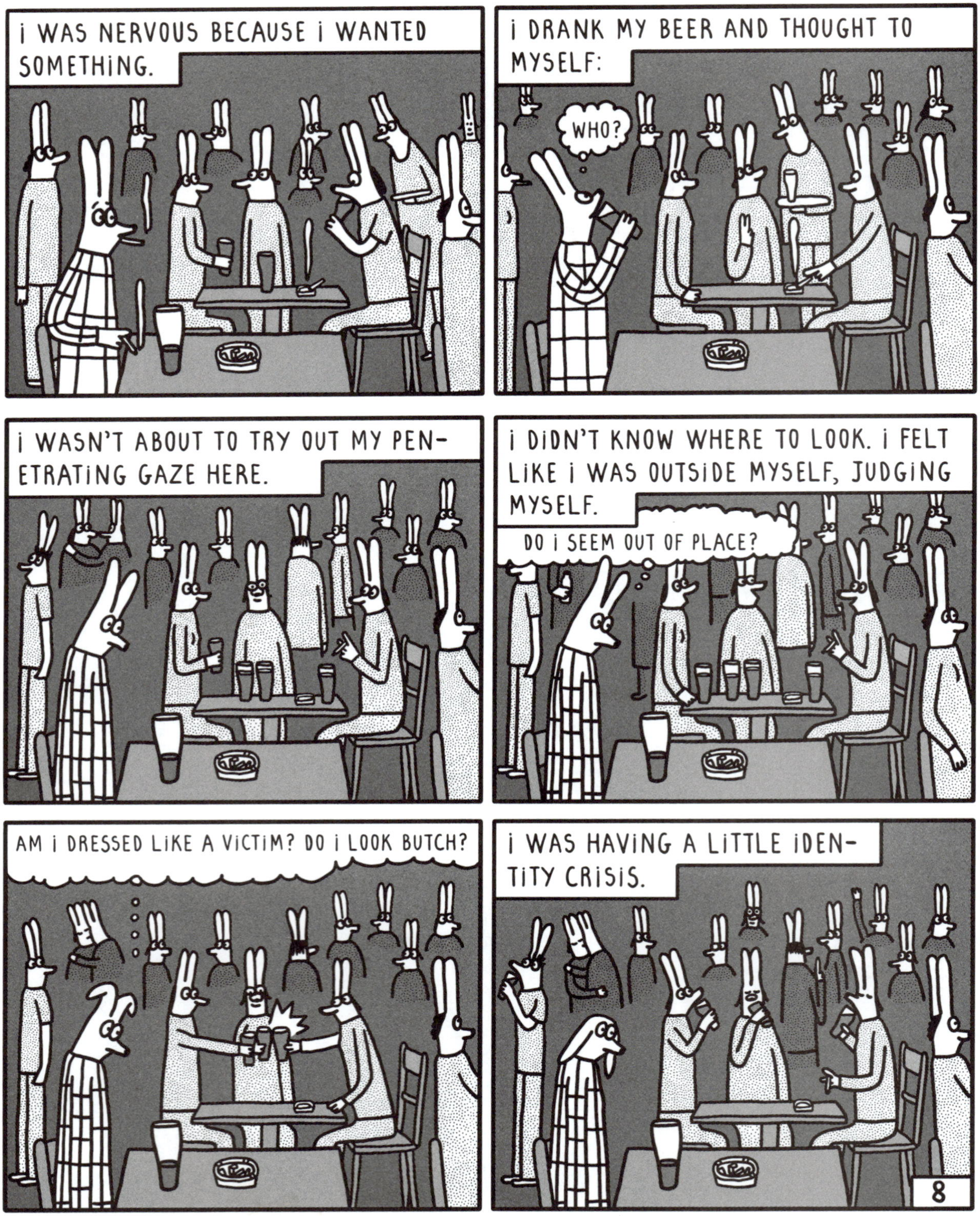
I WAS NERVOUS BECAUSE I WANTED SOMETHING.
I DRANK MY BEER AND THOUGHT TO MYSELF:
WHO?
I WASN'T ABOUT TO TRY OUT MY PEN-ETRATING GAZE HERE.
I DIDN'T KNOW WHERE TO LOOK. I FELT LIKE I WAS OUTSIDE MYSELF, JUDGING MYSELF.
DO I SEEM OUT OF PLACE?
AM I DRESSED LIKE A VICTIM? DO I LOOK BUTCH?
I WAS HAVING A LITTLE IDEN-TITY CRISIS.

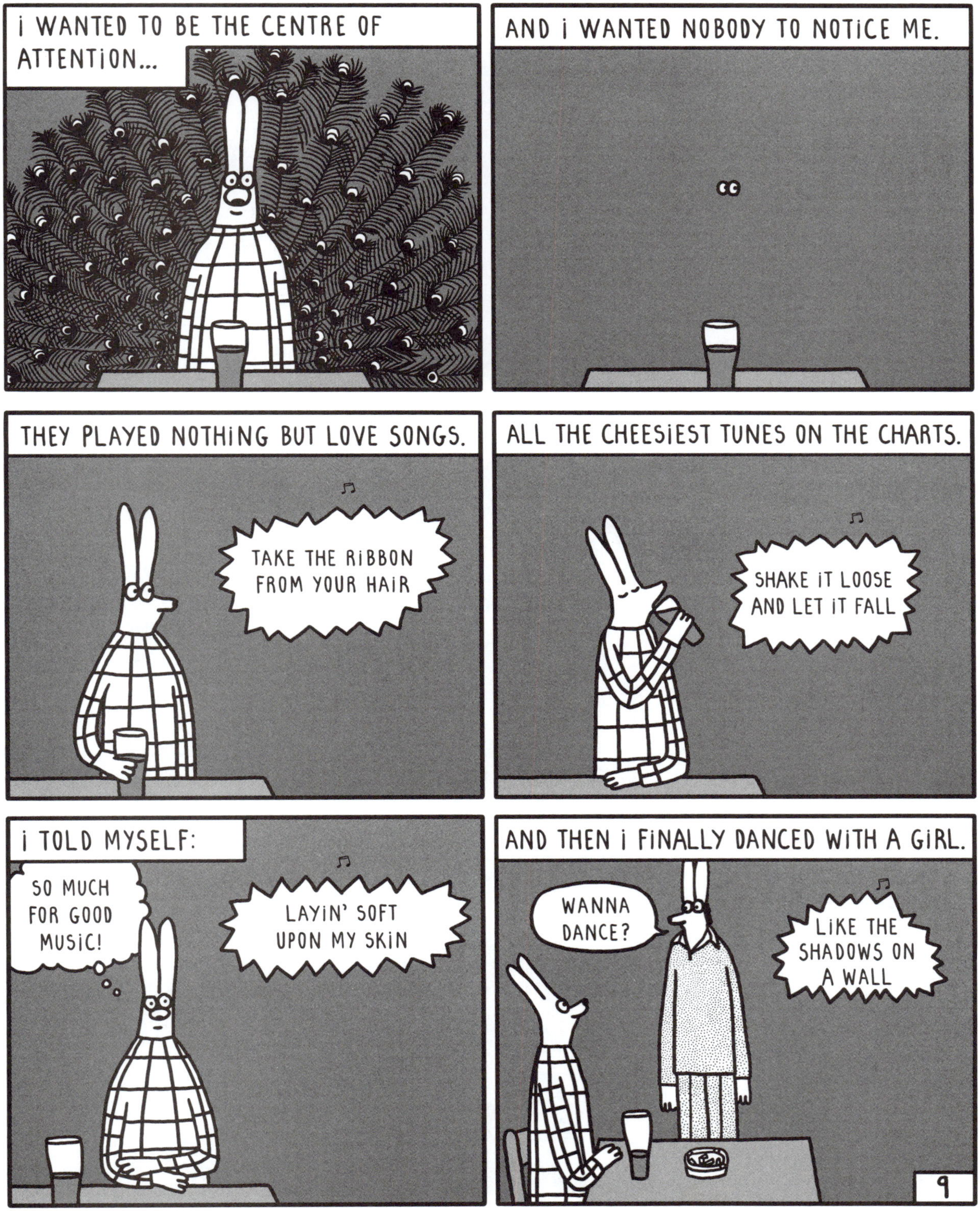

I WANTED TO BE THE CENTRE OF ATTENTION...
AND I WANTED NOBODY TO NOTICE ME.
THEY PLAYED NOTHING BUT LOVE SONGS.
TAKE THE RIBBON FROM YOUR HAIR
ALL THE CHEESIEST TUNES ON THE CHARTS.
SHAKE IT LOOSE AND LET IT FALL
I TOLD MYSELF:
SO MUCH FOR GOOD MUSIC!
LAYIN' SOFT UPON MY SKIN
AND THEN I FINALLY DANCED WITH A GIRL.
WANNA DANCE?
LIKE THE SHADOWS ON A WALL

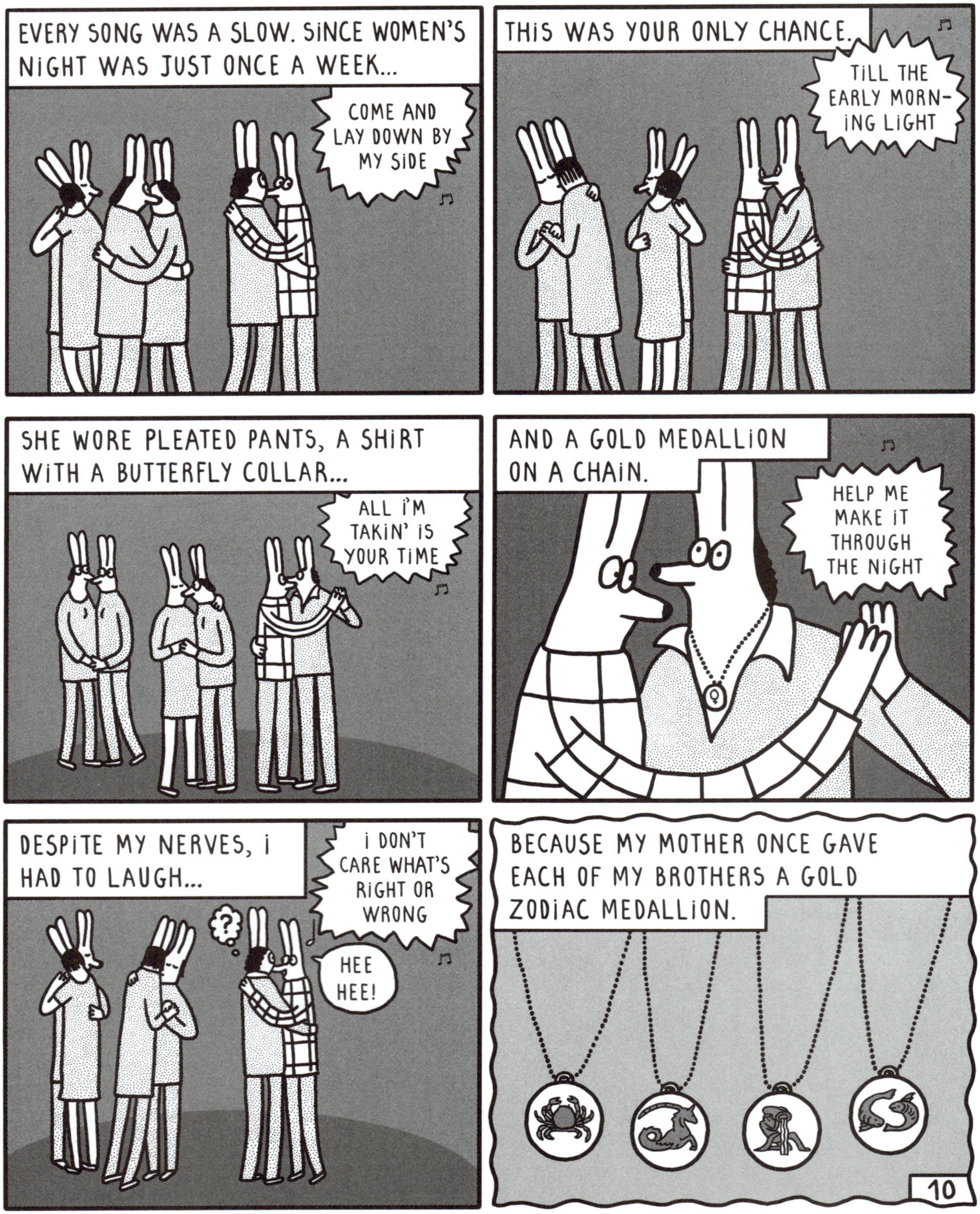
EVERY SONG WAS A SLOW. SINCE WOMEN'S NIGHT WAS JUST ONCE A WEEK...
COME AND LAY DOWN BY MY SIDE
THIS WAS YOUR ONLY CHANCE.
TILL THE EARLY MORNING LIGHT
SHE WORE PLEATED PANTS, A SHIRT WITH A BUTTERFLY COLLAR...
ALL I'M TAKIN' IS YOUR TIME
AND A GOLD MEDALLION ON A CHAIN.
HELP ME MAKE IT THROUGH THE NIGHT
DESPITE MY NERVES, I HAD TO LAUGH...
I DON'T CARE WHAT'S RIGHT OR WRONG
?
HEE HEE!
BECAUSE MY MOTHER ONCE GAVE EACH OF MY BROTHERS A GOLD ZODIAC MEDALLION.

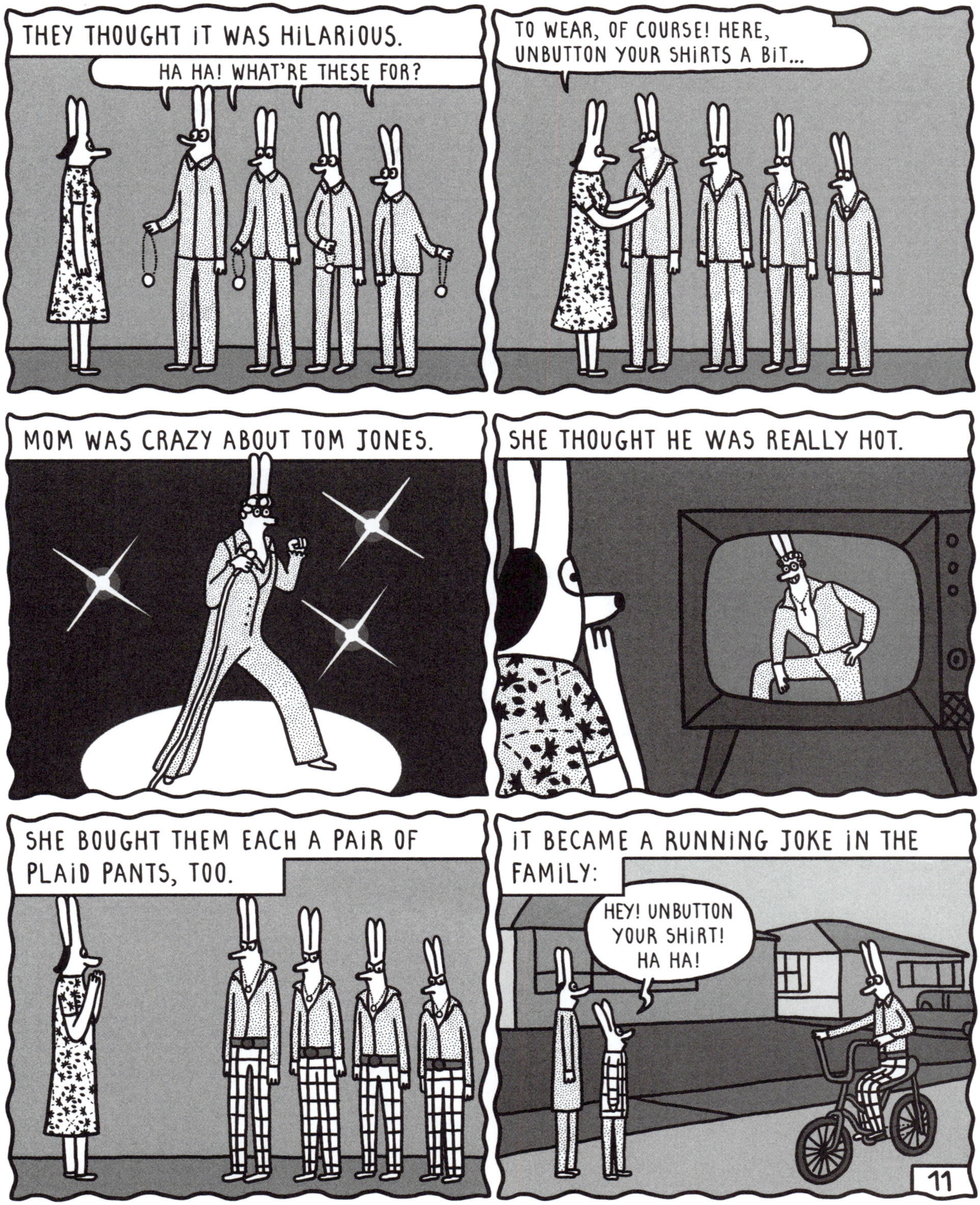
THEY THOUGHT IT WAS HILARIOUS.
HA HA! WHAT'RE THESE FOR?
TO WEAR, OF COURSE! HERE, UNBUTTON YOUR SHIRTS A BIT...
MOM WAS CRAZY ABOUT TOM JONES.
SHE THOUGHT HE WAS REALLY HOT.
SHE BOUGHT THEM EACH A PAIR OF PLAID PANTS, TOO.
IT BECAME A RUNNING JOKE IN THE FAMILY:
HEY! UNBUTTON YOUR SHIRT! HA HA!

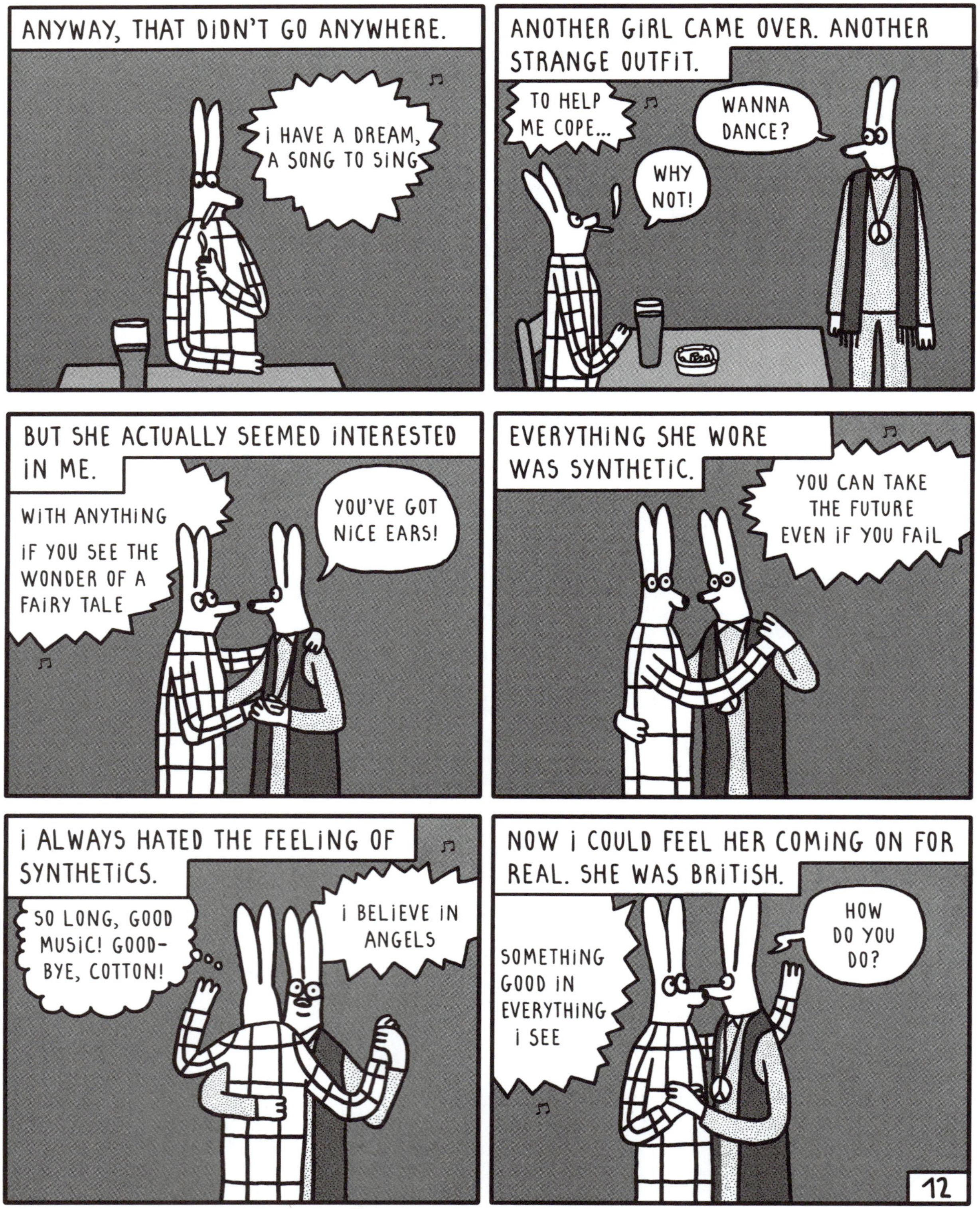
ANYWAY, THAT DIDN'T GO ANYWHERE.
I HAVE A DREAM, A SONG TO SING
ANOTHER GIRL CAME OVER. ANOTHER STRANGE OUTFIT.
TO HELP ME COPE...
WANNA DANCE?
WHY NOT!
BUT SHE ACTUALLY SEEMED INTERESTED IN ME.
WITH ANYTHING
IF YOU SEE THE WONDER OF A FAIRY TALE
YOU'VE GOT NICE EARS!
EVERYTHING SHE WORE WAS SYNTHETIC.
YOU CAN TAKE THE FUTURE EVEN IF YOU FAIL
I ALWAYS HATED THE FEELING OF SYNTHETICS.
SO LONG, GOOD MUSIC! GOOD-BYE, COTTON!
I BELIEVE IN ANGELS
NOW I COULD FEEL HER COMING ON FOR REAL. SHE WAS BRITISH.
SOMETHING GOOD IN EVERYTHING I SEE
HOW DO YOU DO?

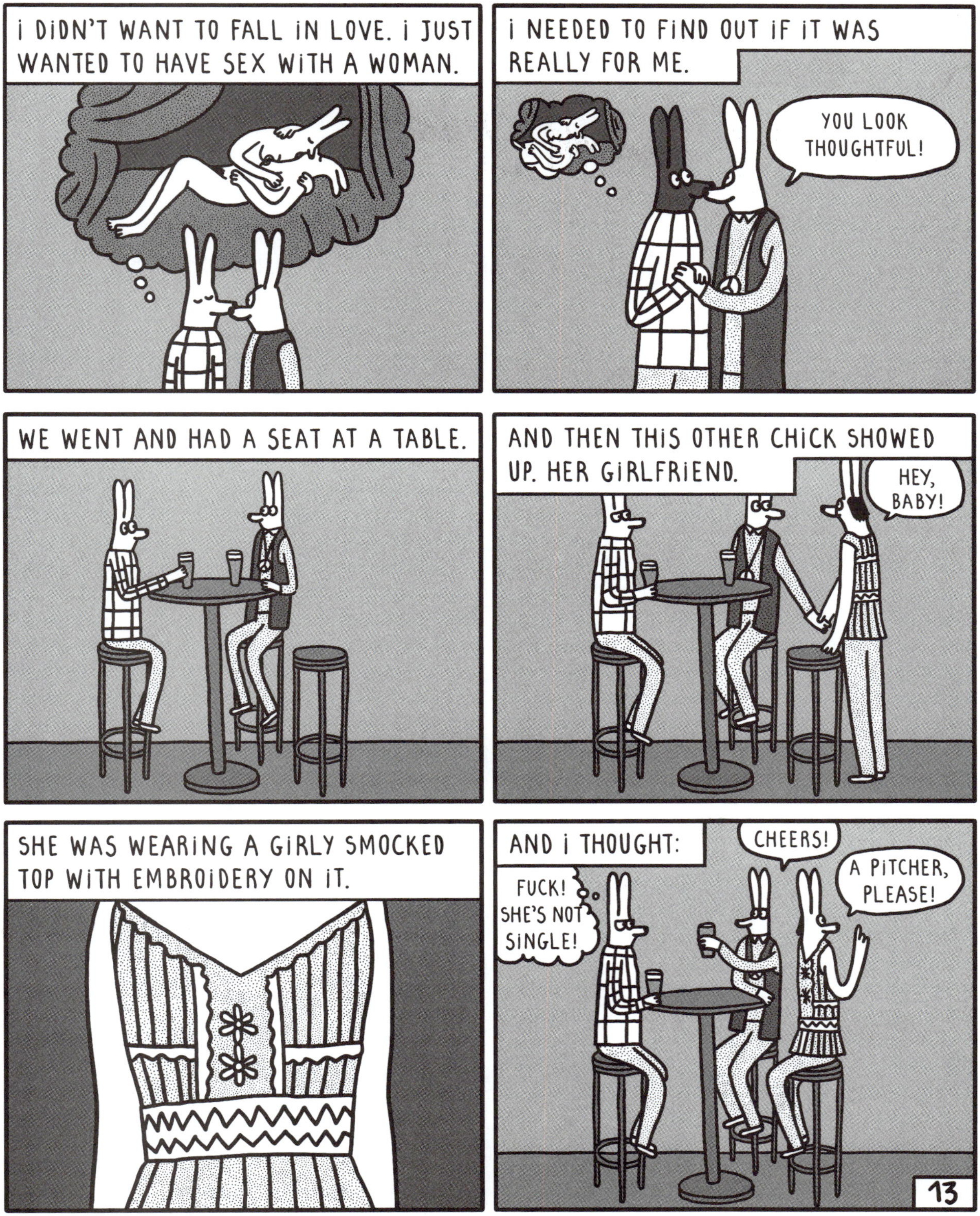
I DIDN'T WANT TO FALL IN LOVE. I JUST WANTED TO HAVE SEX WITH A WOMAN.
I NEEDED TO FIND OUT IF IT WAS REALLY FOR ME.
YOU LOOK THOUGHTFUL!
WE WENT AND HAD A SEAT AT A TABLE.
AND THEN THIS OTHER CHICK SHOWED UP. HER GIRLFRIEND.
HEY, BABY!
SHE WAS WEARING A GIRLY SMOCKED TOP WITH EMBROIDERY ON IT.
AND I THOUGHT:
FUCK! SHE'S NOT SINGLE!
CHEERS!
A PITCHER, PLEASE!

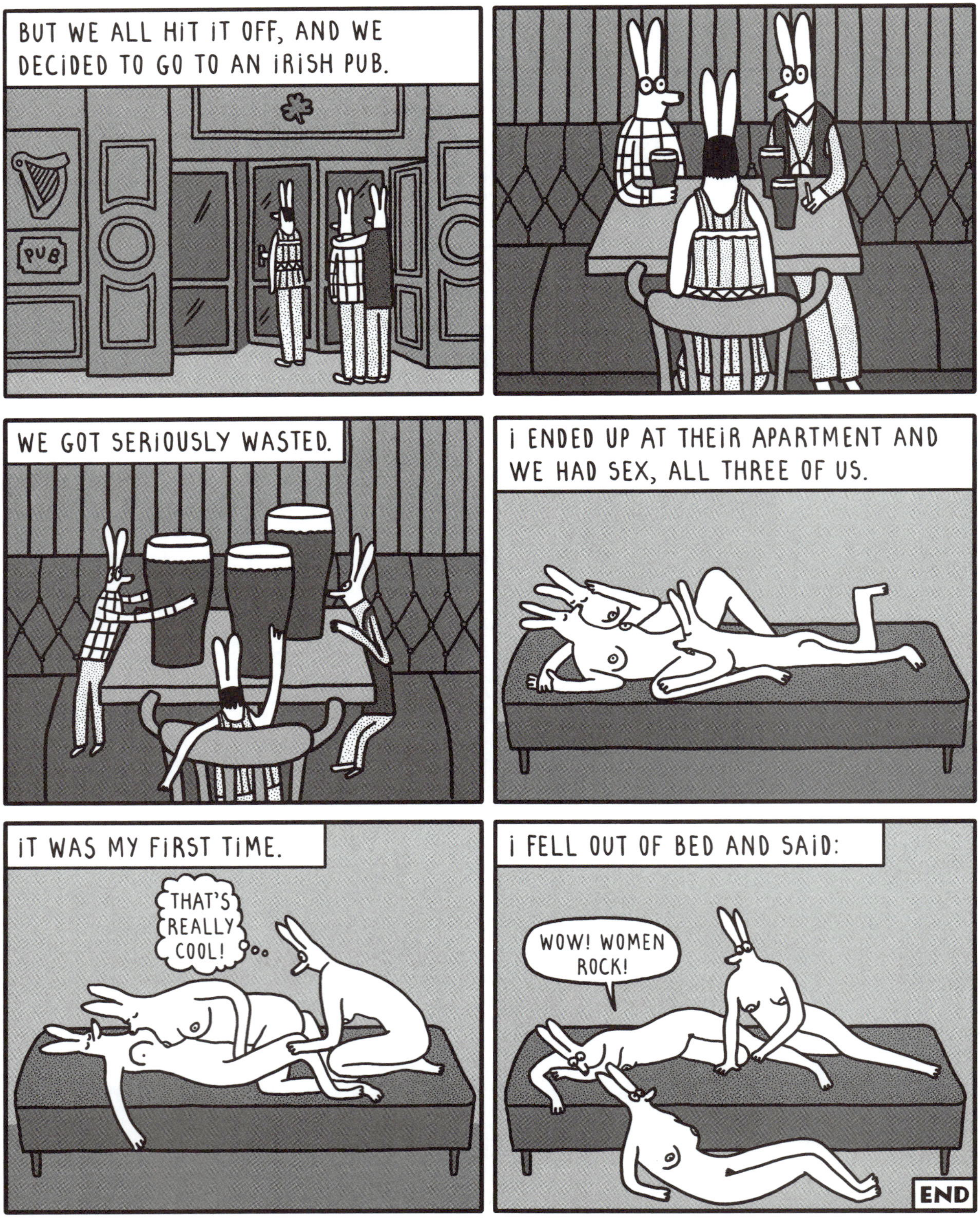
BUT WE ALL HIT IT OFF, AND WE DECIDED TO GO TO AN IRISH PUB.
PUB
WE GOT SERIOUSLY WASTED.
I ENDED UP AT THEIR APARTMENT AND WE HAD SEX, ALL THREE OF US.
IT WAS MY FIRST TIME.
THAT'S REALLY COOL!
I FELL OUT OF BED AND SAID:
WOW! WOMEN ROCK!
END

BORN IN MONTREAL IN 1959, DIANE OBOMSAWIN SPENT
THE FIRST TWENTY YEARS OF HER LIFE IN FRANCE. AFTER
STUDYING GRAPHIC DESIGN, SHE RETURNED TO CANADA
IN 1983 AND TURNED HER ATTENTION TO PAINTING,
COMICS, AND ANIMATION. *HERE AND THERE*, AN
AUTOBIOGRAPHICAL FILM ABOUT THE ARTIST'S ROOTLESS
CHILDHOOD, HAS GARNERED NUMEROUS PRESTIGIOUS
DISTINCTIONS. OVER THE YEARS, OBOMSAWIN HAS
DEVELOPED A UNIQUE STYLE, ACHIEVING A BALANCE
BETWEEN HUMOUR AND SERIOUSNESS, NAÏVETÉ AND
GRAVITAS, REALISM AND POETRY. *ON LOVING WOMEN* IS
HER SECOND BOOK WITH DRAWN & QUARTERLY. HER FIRST,
KASPAR, IS ABOUT THE LIFE OF KASPAR HAUSER; IT WAS
ACCOMPANIED BY A SHORT FILM OF THE SAME NAME.